The F.A. Guide
to Teaching Football

Also by Allen Wade

The F.A. Guide to Training and Coaching

.

The F.A. Guide to Teaching Football

ALLEN WADE

Published on behalf of
THE FOOTBALL ASSOCIATION

HEINEMANN : LONDON

William Heinemann Ltd
15 Queen Street, Mayfair, London W1X 8BE

LONDON   MELBOURNE   TORONTO
JOHANNESBURG   AUCKLAND

First published 1978

434 92210 2

Text set in 10/12 pt VIP Melior, printed by photolithography,
and bound in Great Britain at The Pitman Press, Bath

Contents

V   9–10 Years

Contents

VI 10–11 Years

VII 11–12 Years

X   14–15 Years

XI 15–16 Years

Introduction

Because soccer is the world game it faces problems in schools which are quite unique. A great many schoolboys, some of them very young indeed, have mastered the skills of the game—individual skills and group skills—to levels never attained by their teachers! These relatively high levels of skill have been achieved through the powerful attraction which the game has exerted at three, four, and five years of age following which the game has become a dominant play interest in their lives. In other words the boy, and many more like him, spends a great deal of time playing with a ball with other boys against other boys or alone against a fence or a wall. It is more likely to be the former than the latter. What an intimidating challenge! How can it be possible to teach children who seem to know more than the teacher? This is a very real problem. Unfortunately very few teachers try to solve it.

The majority take the easy way out by letting them get on with it by organizing eleven-a-side games. This is in no one's interest. The majority of children will be uninvolved for long periods, their contact with the ball will be minimal, and they will become bored. Of course the majority of teachers may not aspire to become deeply knowledgeable about soccer. Why should they? But they do have the professional expertise to organize effective practice situations and above all their professional training and experience gives them an insight into the developmental needs of children.

Soccer development like development in other subjects can be simply a matter of setting and solving problems. Clearly the teacher who can set problems and also guide a child towards appropriate solutions has an advantage. But any teacher with imagination can set problems and guide a child towards possible answers. This involves understanding some very simple principles, principles which almost certainly will be within the general experience of any teacher. You don't need to play for England or Brazil or Germany to understand how to stop a moving ball so that it drops softly at your feet. You don't need to be a World Cup star to understand that dribbling is really dodging with a ball at your feet.

This book provides units of work in soccer for the ordinary teacher which cover all the years from seven years of age to sixteen. It has been assumed that soccer occupies both the Autumn and the Spring terms for one games period each week. Each term contains about twelve working weeks and a unit of work has been planned to cover four weeks. There are three units of work for each term and six units for each school year. The distribution of work can be adjusted to meet different working conditions.

Part I indicates the lines which can be followed by the most inexperienced and unknowledgeable teacher, man or woman, who finds himself or herself committed to teaching soccer to children between seven and ten years of age. This is a play-oriented scheme which makes almost no demands on knowledge and very few demands on organization.

Part II covers the years between eight and sixteen and makes slightly greater demands on teacher organization but is still intended for ordinary non-specialist men or women teachers. Skill tests are included which allow sensible practice situations to be created which will challenge the child's interest, which are easily organized and sited, and which progress in degree of difficulty.

While this book has been written as two parts, it has been arranged so that those for whom Part I is most appropriate can easily use relevant units of work in Part II, particularly those prepared for children between eight and ten years of age. Similarly, more knowledgeable teachers will find the simple play-oriented approach in Part I useful in certain circumstances. The units of work presented in Part I for children of seven and eight years of age provide the common starting point for teachers and children.

The Super Skill tests are used as incentives and as progressive tests of developing skill. They are employed towards the end of a term's work, particularly towards the end of the year to give teaching and practice objectivity and purpose. For the same reason the tests used at the end of one year are used during the first unit of work in the following year. In this way the work carries on naturally from one year to the next. Of course the perceptive teacher will use his Super Skill tests to meet the different skill levels of the children.

Tests are designed to meet the needs of children and must be used with flexibility. The reader will note that the Skill Tests are repeated, carrying over the work in one year to the next.

Soccer is easy to teach to children because many of them already know a great deal about it and many are so keen on it. Simple principles, professional organization, appropriate incentive schemes, unlimited encouragement—any teacher worth the name can hardly fail. Even more important, he or she will gain enormous pleasure and satisfaction from the pleasure and satisfaction gained by the children.

ALLEN WADE

Acknowledgements

The Football Association depends upon many people, both paid and unpaid, for the enormous amount of work involved in sustaining and developing the game. I wish to acknowledge here my debt to my colleagues on the Staff of the Education and Coaching Department at The Football Association. They are exemplified best, perhaps, by the senior administrator in the department, Tom Prentice, who has devoted twenty-five years to our cause.

In addition, this book would not have been completed without the dedication of my secretaries Marie Oakerbee and Joan Pritchard or without the exacting artwork undertaken so perceptively by Ian Wade.

Part One

PRINCIPLES OF SOCCER TEACHING

Soccer is a game played between two teams. When one team has the ball they try to score by dribbling it, running with it, kicking it, heading it, and passing it from one player to the other so that finally the ball is played through, past or over opposing players to score a goal. The team which does not have the ball tries to prevent shots towards the goal which it is defending by tackling for the ball, blocking shots, marking dangerous opponents, and by kicking, heading, dribbling or passing the ball away from danger areas near to goal. At the highest level, the game is played by eleven players in a team and there are seventeen simple rules which say how the games will be played. Younger players, however, learn to play the game by playing much smaller sided games with fewer and simpler rules.

To inexperienced teachers and to those who do not know the game, soccer may seem to be a complicated, clever, and highly technical sport. It is true that soccer involves a considerable range of techniques but they need not worry you. The skill of playing soccer is the game itself to which individuals contribute, combining their skills, and exercising imagination and judgement to attack one goal and defend the other.

Soccer teaching, the preparation and organization of lessons and schemes of work, can be complex or simple but there are four principles to be observed by teachers at all levels:

1 Children's interest is best maintained by offering them frequent, planned opportunities to play the game so that each player will have the maximum opportunity to pass, head, dribble, and kick the ball **himself.** The larger the teams the fewer the opportunities to do so. THE SMALLER THE TEAMS THE GREATER THE OPPORTUNITIES FOR INDIVIDUAL DEVELOPMENT.

2 Once the teacher has decided to teach something, he or she alone is responsible for making sure that it is understood, practised, and assessed.

3 Teachers must EVOKE the imagination of children and CHALLENGE their ambition. (The Soccer Star Super Skill Tests which have here been devised should be used for just this purpose.)

4 Finally, teachers must present all games so that analogies can be drawn and demonstrated between good, skilful, and fair play and the integrity, honesty, and fair-mindedness which we are duty bound to inculcate in the minds of children in all social situations.

I

7–9 Years

On your playground or on whatever playing space you have mark
out, if possible, one 'grid' area 60 yards × 60 yards. At the very least
the grid should be 60 yards × 40 yards. A grid is any area, such as
one of those already mentioned, sub-divided into 10 yards × 10
yards squares. One grid square (10 yards × 10 yards) provides a
useful practice area for a small group of boys—two, three or even
four—depending upon their levels of skill. Even more importantly,
single squares can be combined with others to form progressively
larger playing 'pitches' for 2 v 2 or 3 v 3 games (fig. 1) Goals can be
improvised by using posts in bases or the plastic cones which are
used as markers on motorways. It is better, however, if miniature
goals with nets can be provided (16 feet wide × 4 feet high). They
provide a tremendous incentive for children and players of all ages
and practice attitudes are improved out of all recognition by proper
goals. They are worth the trouble and the expense; and so are
brightly coloured, distinctive team bibs.

Lesson Plan for 7 year olds

Number of children: 20 plus
Number of large plastic balls (with spotted
markings if possible):   20 plus
Number of posts, skittles or 'cones':   12
Time: 30–40 minutes

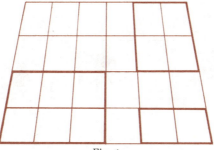

Fig. 1

Introductory Activities

In pairs, one ball between two, two players to two grid squares. Keep the ball in your own area all the time.
1 Kick the ball to each other so that:
the ball rolls all along the ground
or the ball lifts off the ground
or the ball spins (turns)—the teacher suggests different directions of spin.

2 When the ball is kicked to you, you may **stop it using any part of your body** to keep it on your pitch. As your partner's kicks become better controlled try to stop them with any part of your body **except your hands or arms.** Later still try to stop the ball using:
your legs and feet only
your body **above your waist** if the ball bounces high enough
your **head** if it bounces higher still
your **feet** only
your **chest** and so on.

3. Remaining in your pitch (2 squares), make sure you stay within the boundary lines. Dribble the ball anywhere within the pitch trying to prevent your partner taking it away from you.

How many times can you touch the ball **with either foot** before he takes the ball away from you? How long can you keep the ball by dribbling it with **the same foot all the time**?
Running with the ball within your pitch, while your partner rests, how many **different ways** can you find **of changing direction**?
Still practising in your two squares (pitch) one of you starts in one square with the ball while your partner waits in the other square (fig. 2). Player A tries to dribble the ball into player B's square, past B and onto the goal line behind him. **You must play within your pitch boundary lines all the time.**

Fig. 2

Children benefit most from practice involving as much contact
with a ball as possible. They are inclined to be selfish. Don't worry, it
is not normal or natural for children to understand the need for
unselfishness and for serious and knowledgeable team play until
they are twelve or thirteen years of age. **Encourage good control and
cleverness.**

Game: 2 v 2

Divide the class into teams of 2. Try to partner the better players and
the stronger players with the not so skilful and the not so strong
children.

2 v 2 games, for children of this age, should be played on a pitch
which is 20 yards long × 20 yards wide (4 Grid Squares). No need to
bother about goalkeepers as such although one player on each team
can be allowed to handle the ball to prevent goals being scored.

If the ball goes out of play the game should be restarted with a roll
in rather than with a proper throw in or a corner kick.

What do you need to know to teach boys when they are playing 2
a-side soccer?

1. If your partner has the ball and can kick (pass) it forward (towards
your opponent's goal) easily, run past opponents to meet his pass
and try to score.

2. If your partner can't pass the ball forward easily move into a part
of the pitch where (if he wants to) he can pass to you.

3. When dribbling past an opponent try to do it so that you can then shoot OR so that you can give an accurate pass to your team mate.

That's enough information for the present. If you can encourage children to do those things mentioned so far, more successfully, if you can also evoke their imagination and their enthusiasm for play and practice, you are more than half way towards producing the best sort of experience for the next generation of skilful players.

Game: 3 v 3

Boys between 7 and 8 or 9 years of age should play a lot of two or three a-side soccer and, at the most, five a-side. In fact three a-side is the real foundation of all soccer. Again, no goalkeeper needed but perhaps one handling player.

In addition to points 1–3 in the 2 v 2 game, practise the following techniques:

1. Try to find positions where your partners can pass the ball to you easily, if they need to, and where you can also—
shoot effectively
dribble successfully
pass accurately
… IF and WHEN you get the ball.

2. If your two team mates are moving forward by interpassing or dribbling successfully **follow them up (support them)** (fig. 3).

3. **Shoot** when you can see the goal and when you think you can hit it more often than not.
If your team loses the ball either:

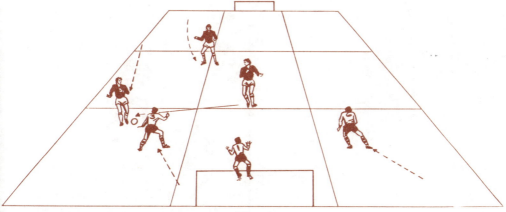

Fig. 3

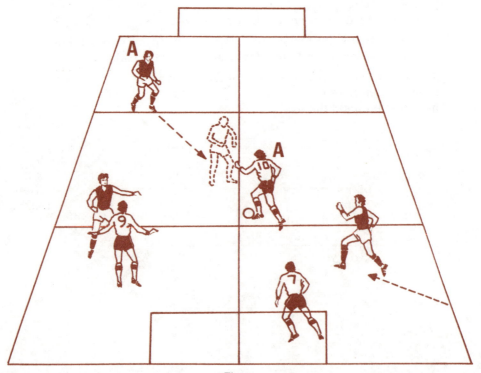

Fig. 4

challenge (tackle) the opponent who has the ball if no one else looks
like doing it, or
get behind (cover) a team mate who is challenging for the ball.
Prevent opponents from shooting, if they look like doing so, by
blocking their shots.

Fig. 5

4. TAKE CARE, WHATEVER YOU ARE DOING, TO AVOID PLAY
WHICH MAY BE DANGEROUS TO AN OPPONENT OR TO ONE OF
YOUR OWN PLAYERS. DANGEROUS PLAY IS UNSKILFUL PLAY.

In fig. 4, where white A has the ball, for the moment A and C are in
shooting positions. B only needs to follow up (support) and watch to
see how he can help them **if** they need help.

In fig. 5, white A may shoot and so black A, the nearest opponent,
must challenge to prevent (block) the shot.

In fig. 6, where black A is in a dangerous position and where white
A is challenging, white B's position behind (covering) A is a sensible
one.

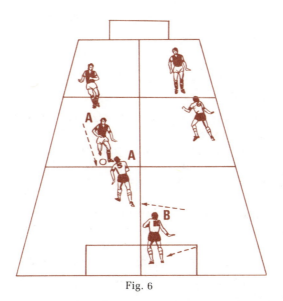

Fig. 6

Soccer, whether 3 a-side or 11 a-side, basically is about spaces and
triangles but don't worry about it. The whole business will become
clear if you are willing to watch and to think about the basic
propositions involved in defending and attacking.

II

9–10 Years

Basic Games

1. 2 v 2 on a 20 yards × 20 yards square or, **for more skilful players** on a 20 yards × 10 yards square.

In simple terms, the most skilful players will respond better to restricted spaces, not so skilful players will continue to need reasonably large spaces and unskilful players may need larger spaces still.

For similar reasons the more skilful players will master (and learn from the mastery of) smaller balls while less skilful players respond better to a larger ball.

2. 3 v 3 on a 30 yards × 30 yards OR 30 yards × 20 yards pitch.

3. 4 v 4 on a 40 yards × 40 yards OR 40 yards × 30 yards pitch.

Lesson Plan for 9 year olds

Number of children:	20 plus
Number of plastic balls of different sizes:	20 plus
Number of posts or skittles:	12 and 3 sets of small goals.
A Coaching grid.	
Time:	30–40 minutes.

Introductory Activities

In pairs, one ball between two, two players to a 3 squares pitch. Each player stands in one of the end squares leaving one empty square between them. (fig. 7).

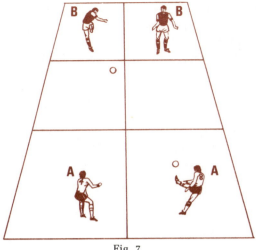

Fig. 7

A kicks to B and B to A, each player must remain in his own square all the time. The ball must never leave the pitch.

Activity 1
Keep the ball on the ground all the time.
How many **different parts of your foot** can you use to pass the ball to your partner?
Can you pass the ball effectively using **all** the different ways?
Effect will be judged by:

the ease with which the ball can be passed when the passer has used only one touch to control it.
or the ease with which the ball can be passed first time—with no extra controlling touch.
or the variation in pace which the passer can use easily.

Any passing technique which does not appear to offer reasonable possibilities for the points mentioned above may be a technique which is not worth practising!

Activity 2
The ball must move from one end square to the other but it **must not touch the empty square between.**
Can you kick the ball to your partner so that it spins backwards in the air?
or sideways in the air?

Can you kick the ball so that it spins and swerves?
or rises as steeply as possible?
or dips in the air?
Initially, allow the receiving player to catch the ball like a goal-keeper, if he wishes to do so.

Practise the following points for goalkeeping:

1. position your hands to the side of and behind the ball
2. allow your hands to give slightly with the impact
3. keep your body or your head (eyes) behind the ball
4. allow no gaps between your feet or knees through which the ball can slip
5. later, impose restrictions on the stopping techniques to be used
6. use the inside of your foot only
7. use the sole of your foot just as the ball strikes the ground
8. stop the ball using the top of your foot
9. stop the ball with your thigh, chest or head

You may find it useful to challenge children by setting the following problems.

Can you stop the ball so suddenly that it remains dead within three feet of your first contact position?

Can you stop the ball so that you actually catch it on your foot, your thigh, your chest or your head?

If 3 v 3 games are used as the small game basis for practice, the following teaching points are appropriate at this stage.

When your team has the ball:

1. get as far away from your opponents as you can;
if you can move behind them without being noticed so much the better!
2. if the player who has the ball looks like losing it to an opponent, go towards him so that he can pass to you if he wants to
3. if you are the player with the ball try to play it past an opponent by dribbling or tricking him
or by running past him quickly
or by passing to a team mate
so that someone on your team has a chance for a shot at goal.

When your team hasn't the ball:

1. stand close to (mark) your nearest opponent between him and your goal; when he tries to dodge away from you mark him closely

2. try to prevent your opponent from passing effectively or shooting accurately

3. in your team play try different ways of preventing him from getting the ball past you by making a tight triangle pattern to present a barrier in front of him

or by moving or dodging about in front of him so that he is not sure when or if you will try to tackle for the ball.

or by moving away from him (retreating) if he is a faster runner than you, until he makes a mistake in his ball control and you can take the ball away from him.

4 v 4 Games

You may continue to use a handling player OR have a goalkeeper. Try to ensure that everyone has experience in goal. If a handling player is used, that is to say all four players may move freely around the pitch, the fourth player positions himself to produce **an extra triangle**.

In fig. 8 players A, B and C have formed a triangle passing pattern for the fourth player D. Any one of the two alternative D positions makes good positional sense for B who has the ball.

Triangle play is the best way of positioning yourselves to give good all-round passing chances and also good supporting positions in most circumstances.

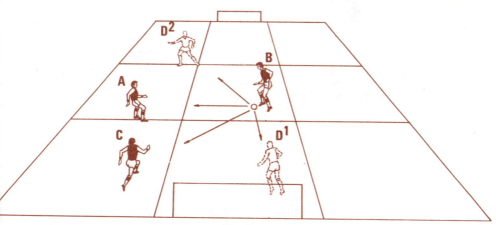

Fig. 8

Space. You don't need to play for England to understand that the closer **all** or **most** of the players in both teams position themselves

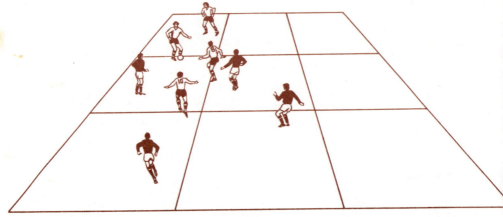

Fig. 9

to each other, the greater the difficulty they will all have in controlling and passing the ball.

In fig. 9 the white players who are bunched together will NEVER play skilful football. They haven't the SPACE and therefore they haven't the TIME.

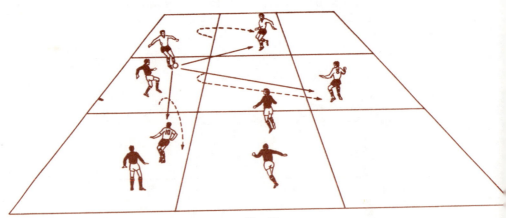

Fig. 10

SPACE IS TIME IN FOOTBALL.

In fig. 10 the players have spread out and made more space in the pattern of play. Each player now will have more time. He will see the game better and he will enjoy it more because of the time and space he now has in which to use his skill.

When your team has the ball ask yourself:

1. Am I in a position which will help the player with the ball to pass in as many directions as possible, if he wants to?

2. How far away from my opponents can I position myself so that the player with the ball can still pass to me if he wishes to do so? To make a good pass or to stop the ball effectively, make contact with the ball, or allow the ball to make contact with you, **exactly where you want contact to be made.** This means that you must pay attention to making an absolutely accurate contact. As you become more skilful you will seem to pay less attention! This is because good techniques have become habits. When the ball misbehaves, or seems to have a mind of its own, this is your fault and not the ball's. You must concentrate more on what you want to do and what you want the ball to do.

When the opposing team has the ball:

1. Be patient in trying to get the ball away from them. Never tackle a tricky or speedy player until you are sure of winning the ball. Running at him or towards him may help him to beat you.

2. Be near enough to an opponent so that you have a chance to intercept the ball or tackle for it if the ball is passed to him.

3. Unless you are outnumbered never allow opponents space in which they can take their time in choosing what to do.

III

---

10 Years

Basic Games

1 v 1 up to 5 v 5.
6 v 6 may be played if one player is the goalkeeper.

Six a-side Soccer is a fully recognized indoor game played by men and often played by professional footballers. Technique and judgement developed in playing small sided games is vitally important in the development of high standards of soccer skill. A poor 5 or 6 a-side schoolboy player will rarely if ever make a successful international player at any level.

Lesson Plan

Number of players:	20–40 plus.
Number of balls:	10–20
Number of posts or skittles:	18
Portable small goals:	4 sets
A coaching grid.	
Time:	30–40 minutes

Introductory Activities

1. Three players with one ball to one square. Remaining within the square and keeping the ball inside the square all the time practise: continuous ground passing in one direction using two touches—one

to control the ball, the second to pass
as previously but change the direction of passing flow and use your other foot
as previously but more freely within the square and interchange positions by moving across the square as well as round it.

2. Three players to a square with one ball. Free passing around the square but keep the ball in the air. The ball may be allowed to bounce no more than twice before being played by the next player. Later allow one bounce only.
Any part of the body, other than the hand or arm, can be used to pass the ball.

3. Two against one in two squares. A throws to B avoiding C. B must control the ball while it is in the air and catch it before it touches the ground or before C can intercept it. If C intercepts the ball or if A or B allow the ball to pass outside the square, the player who made the mistake must take the place of the player in the middle and the game continues—throw, control, catch and so on.

5 v 5 or 6 v 6 Games

These games should be played on a pitch 40 yards × 40 yards or 40 yards × 30 yards. (The higher the skill the smaller the pitch and vice versa).

   In fig. 11 while white players A, B, C, D and E are spread out well, the opposing players are effectively filling spaces which are needed by whites if they are to attack and score.

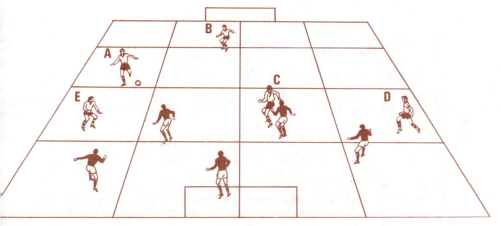

Fig. 11

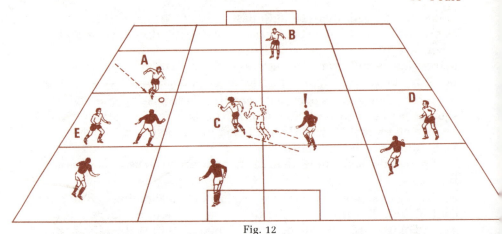

Fig. 12

In fig. 12 the movement of C back towards goal and towards A sets a problem for his nearest opponent. Should he follow C and leave a space in the middle of the field, perhaps finding A and C combining against him? Or should he hold his position and allow C to have almost complete freedom to receive the ball and set up an attacking movement?

Creating similar situations, making space, setting opponents marking problems, exploiting space or two against one advantages are at the very foundations of soccer thinking.

How can problems be solved? Only by improving technical skill, cleverness in passing or dribbling and by playing with more patience and accuracy when manoeuvring for shooting space within the danger area near to goal.

Problems to be presented to players:
1. How can defenders be drawn (tempted) away from goal?
2. How can defenders be disturbed in their positional relationships with each other?
3. How can attackers run at and past opponents into good shooting areas?
4. How can a team keep possession of the ball while trying to make 'two against one' situations near to an opponent?

It all sounds complicated but it isn't really. Finding solutions to these basic games problems is just as fascinating for the non-player as it is for the great international and they are fundamental to all team passing games.

Part Two

YEAR-BY-YEAR TRAINING

In Part 2 we are concerned with those teachers who have some knowledge, some skill and a lot of ambition to teach rather more than the most elementary aspects of soccer. At the same time the aim is to present teaching possibilities which still cater for the needs of the non-expert teacher and certainly for the capabilities of both men and women teachers. The lesson pattern will be as follows:

1. *Introductory Activities*
Practice of known or of simply organized activities which are interesting.
or Practice of activities which require little organization and into which CHALLENGE can be easily injected.

2. *Class Activities*
A new or relatively new activity in which all or one half of the class can take part and which contains a teaching objective of enough importance to warrant it being taught to a large number at the same time.

3. *Group Practices*
Practices which are quickly organized and which are easily sited. These practices **must** be challenging and, preferably, involve objective tests which are simple to administer.
The tests which are used in this book, the Super Star Super Skill tests, have been designed and standardized to meet the needs of the average child (though every teacher knows there is no such thing as the 'average child'). The test scores shown throughout each group of tests are those which are recommended as starting points for the child. The tests and the recommended scores can be adjusted to meet the needs of those who are gifted and those who are less gifted.

4. *Final Activities*

These activities for the whole class may be similar to the introductory activities or they may be small-sided games.

IV

8–9 Years

Unit 1

The following scheme of work, covering one year, is prepared for two school terms (28 weeks). Each **unit** of work will last for 4–5 weeks. Units of work are to be regarded as frameworks only. The development and progress of the children will control the change from one unit to the next.

Number in Class: 40 plus
Area: playground preferably or a field.
60 yards × 40 yards or 60 yards × 60 yards marked out as a grid in 10 yards × 10 yards squares.
Equipment: spotted plastic balls—one ball to two children. 16 posts in bases or 16 plastic cones (similar to those used on motorways).
coloured team braids (or bibs).
Time: 60 minutues.

It cannot be emphasized enough that light portable goals, 16 feet × 4 feet high, with nets, are invaluable not only because **the game needs goals** but because of the enormous enthusiasm which **shooting into a real goal** will provoke. Make-do goals are often necessary but they are just not the same.

Introductory Activities (10 minutes)

Find a partner and number yourselves one and two.
Find your own square in the grid.
Number ones fetch a ball.
Keeping your ball inside your square all the time—pass the ball to your partner using ANY part of your body to do so.
When the ball comes to you make sure you stop it inside your square.
How many different ways can you pass the ball?

During this activity try to practise the following points:

Strike through the fattest part of the ball along an imaginary line straight to your partner.
Look to see exactly where you hit the ball.
Strike the ball so that it doesn't turn or spin or if it does turn so that it only rolls forward.
How many different ways can you find to stop the ball?
How many ways can you find to stop it without using your hands or arms?

Practise the following:

Try to imagine the line along which the ball will come to you. Position yourself at the end of that line. As the ball approaches you, allow whatever part of your body you are using to stop the ball, to give with it, and to cushion it, so that it drops softly to the ground. It is easier and safer to use a big stopping surface than a small one.

Can you dribble the ball round your square using your feet only, staying inside the square all the time?

Keep the ball moving. Vary your running speed from slow to fast. Imagine you are tricking your opponents while you are dribbling.

In fig. 13, starting in one corner, with your partner in the middle of the square, try to dribble the ball across the square past your partner to finish in the far corner. Then change over.

Practise the following:

Use the top, outside part of your foot to dribble with (the part of your shoe above your three little toes). Stay close to the ball all the time.

Keep your ankles and feet fairly loose and relaxed as you push the ball forward.

Be prepared to take advantage of any move by your opponent to enable you to move off in a different direction and past him.

Fig. 13

Class Activities (20 minutes)

Half the class practise passing and stopping, as in the introductory activities.

The other half practise dribbling as in the introductory activities. Change over after 10 minutes.

Game (20 minutes)
Use posts or cones to mark the corners of a 20 yards × 20 yards (4 squares) pitch (fig. 14).

2 v 2 football matches. With a large class (40 plus) and a 60 yards × 40 yards grid only half the class can play at the same time. The problem can be solved by having 4 teams (8 players) to each pitch.

With well disciplined young players, A and C teams play B and D teams at CHANGE soccer as follows:

Teams A and B begin the game while the C and D teams are off the pitch. On a signal (whistle) A and B stop playing and run off leaving the ball wherever it happens to be while teams C and D run on and take up the game where A and B left off. The combined scores of A and C and of B and D produce the final result.

Final Activities

Use one of the introductory activities as a final activity and re-emphasize one of the techniques.

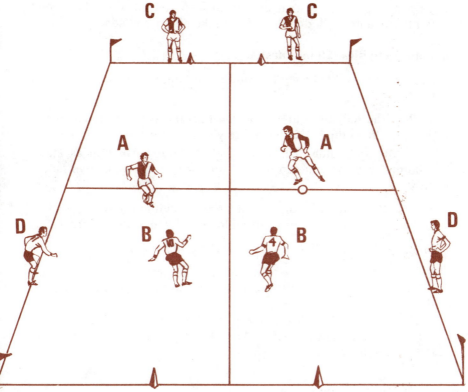

Fig. 14

Unit 2

Introductory Activities (5–10 minutes)

1. One ball between two, two players to one grid square. One player, keeping inside the square all the time, dribbles the ball freely. His partner follows behind (shadows) as closely as he can. The first player tries to twist and turn, while dribbling to lose his shadow. On the whistle the dribbling player puts his foot on the ball, stops it and leaves it for his shadow. The positions are now reversed and practice continues accordingly.

2. In pairs, one ball between two, in one square, try different ways of passing the ball to your partner and different ways of stopping it.

In both activities practise the following points:

Control the ball using the outside and the inside of either foot. This will allow twists and turns with the ball to be carried out more easily.

Vary the speed of your dribbling to lose your shadow. Use body feints (pretend to dodge) to try to shake off your shadow.

Class Activities (20 minutes)

In pairs, one ball between two and remaining inside your square all the time:

1. Pass the ball to your partner so that the ball never leaves the ground. When the ball is passed to you stop it using your foot only.

2. Throw and catch. Throw the ball to your partner in as many different ways as you can using—one or two hands, or two hands only.

Your partner must be able to catch the ball without moving his feet and without changing his position for a throw to count as successful.

Practise the Football Throw during these activities:

Stand with your feet apart—forwards or sideways it doesn't matter.
    Place your hands (with fingers spread) to the side of and behind the ball.
    The ball must be released over your head.
    Half the class practise Class Activity 1 and the other half practise Class Activity 2.

Group Practice (20 minutes)

Divide the class into 4 groups. Send each group to a part of the grid or to a specific area of the playground or field.
Each group practises one of the following activities:

1. Passing and stopping—use different ways to stop the ball except your hands or arms. Stop the ball so that it drops at your feet.

2. Dribbling

3. Passing to keep the ball on the ground—stopping it with your feet only. Stop the ball so that you can give a return pass as quickly as possible.

4. Soccer Throw. Each player throws in turn to his partner who stops the ball using any part of his body and passes it back along the ground to the first player.

Final Activity

Dribbling to lose your shadow as previously.

Unit 3

Introductory Activities (10 minutes)

1. Dribbling to lose your shadow, and/or
2. Practise the Soccer Throw In in pairs—stop the ball and pass it back along the ground as accurately and as quickly as you can.
   Practise ball control and dribbling as in Unit 2.

Class Activities (10 minutes)

In pairs the first player stands with feet wide apart (wide enough for the ball to pass through). His partner passes the ball, keeping the ball on the ground all the time, so that it travels between the target player's feet without touching them. Change over. During this activity:

swing your foot through the ball along the imaginary line which passes between your partner's feet,
strike the ball through its fattest part,
make sure that you can balance easily on your standing foot when striking the ball.

Group Practices (20 minutes)

Groups change stations every five minutes, each group doing one of the following:

1. passing and stopping—different ways
2. dribbling round your partner
3. passing the ball through your partner's legs, keeping the ball on the ground all the time
4. Football Throw—for distance and accuracy.

Game (20 minutes)

Four teams of two on a 4 squares pitch practise Change Soccer. Two against two, the teams change over on a signal.

Note the following points:

When you think that your partner can pass the ball behind an opponent be prepared to run there for it. If your partner is trying to dribble past an opponent, help him by positioning yourself so that he can pass to you if he wishes to do so. This is known as supporting him. Shoot when you can hit the target.

In these games, activity is more important than game patterns. The games may seem crude and play may appear to be disorganized. Players will be selfish in keeping the ball. **This doesn't matter as long as they become better at keeping it!**

Final Activity

One ball between two, in one square.

Soccer throws to your partner so that the ball bounces once only before he catches it.

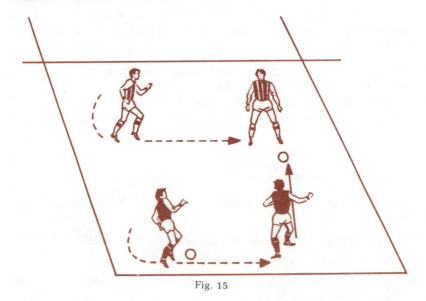

Fig. 15

Unit 4

Introductory Activities (5–10 minutes)

In pairs, one ball between two, in one square (fig. 15). The first player runs freely anywhere inside the square dribbling the ball. His partner, whenever he chooses to do so, stops suddenly with feet

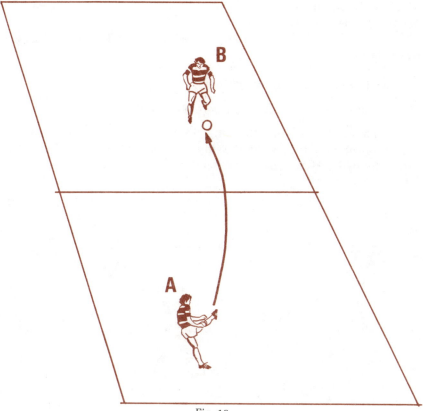

Fig. 16

wide apart. After his partner stands still the player with the ball is allowed three touches to pass the ball between his partner's feet. Later, reduce the number of touches within which the pass must be made until, as soon as his partner shows the target position, the first player must try to pass through the 'target' player's feet.

Class Activity (10 minutes)

In pairs working along two squares, one player in each square, A kicks the ball to B so that, when passing over the mid-line, the ball is in the air (fig. 16). The ball and the players must remain within their two square pitch all the time. B must stop the ball inside his own square before returning the kick to A, over the mid-line.

The following should be practised:

kick with the tops of your toes or the bottom laces of your shoes
strike the ball below its fattest part
kick through the ball swinging your foot along an imaginary line to
your target

Group Practices (30 minutes)

Each group practises one of the following activities:

1. In pairs, passing and stopping. Find different ways of passing
and stopping the ball without using your hands and arms. Can you
stop the ball and pass back accurately
in   3 touches?
or in   2 touches?
or in   1 touch?

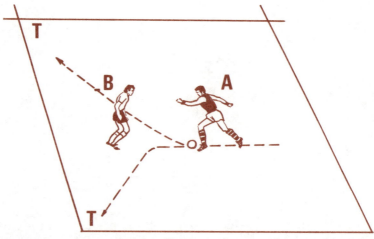

Fig. 17

2. Dribbling. In fig. 17, player A starts on the line with the ball and
tries to dribble past B into either one or the other of the target
corners, T. How many successes out of three tries?
   Change over dribbler A and defender B after every three attempts.

3. In pairs, one ball, in one square. Free running and dribbling. As
soon as A makes a wide astride target, B must try to score between
A's feet
in   3 touches?
or in   2 touches?
or in   1 touch?

4. Football Throw for distance and accuracy—competition.

Fig. 18

5. Four players, one ball, in one or two squares (fig. 18).

3 v 1, 'Keep Ball'. Can you make 20, 15, 10 uninterrupted passes before the player in the middle touches the ball or causes it to leave the pitch?

6. Two players to a square. Each player has a ball. 'Bounce Ball'—use any part of your body, including your hands or arms, to keep a sequence of bounces going. If you use your hand or arm you must use a different part of your body for the next bounce. The ball is allowed to bounce on the ground once only between each body bounce.

The practice groups change stations every five minutes.

Final Activity (5 minutes)

Using the whole grid, 60 yards × 40 yards or 60 yards × 60 yards, the ball is not allowed to leave the pitch. Six players put on coloured braids.

The remaining players try to build up an unbroken sequence of 20 passes.

When the target of successive passes is achieved another player puts on a coloured braid and the remainder again attempt to build up an unbroken target sequence.

Carry on adding opponents until the sequence of passes rarely, if ever, exceeds 10.

Fig. 19

Unit 5

Introductory Activity (5 minutes)

In pairs, one ball between two, working over two squares (fig. 19).
Imagine that the mid-line between the two squares is a net. Each pair
tries to build up a long sequence of passes across the net as in tennis.
Before being played back over the net the ball may bounce twice but
a player may choose to play the ball back across the net after the first
bounce or even before it bounces at all.

Class Activities (10 minutes)

1. In 4's working in one square with one ball, three against one,
practise Keep Ball.

If three playing against one in one square cannot establish sequences of 10–20 passes they should return to the two square pitch. Some players may be skilful enough to play two against one in a single square.

Practise the following points:

Use the corners of the square as much as you can to make wide angles for the player with the ball.

If you are not passing the ball or receiving a pass or preparing to receive a pass, find a position in which you will be an easy target for a subsequent pass.

Passing practices must always allow for the possibility of the player with the ball pretending to pass and then dribbling past his opponent. Soccer skill, real soccer skill, depends upon a player's ability to trick opponents and to disguise or hide his intentions.

2. In pairs, working in one square with one ball (fig. 20). Player A, holding the ball in two hands, pulls the ball onto his forehead at the same time nodding the ball out of his hands towards his partner, player B.

Practise the following points:

Strike the ball with the flat part of the forehead above the eyebrows. Nod through the fattest part of the ball towards your target.

Fig. 20

Spread your feet forwards and backwards so that you can swing your body backwards and forwards to add power to your nodding (heading) movement.

Group Practices—Green Star Super Skill Tests

1. *Touch Test—juggling*
Standing and remaining inside a 10 yard square throw the ball into the air. Allow it to bounce on the ground and use any part of your body, including your hand or arm, to start a bouncing sequence going. After using your hand or arm once, you must use a different part of your body for the next bounce.

Score: 6 bounces in succession.

2. *Heading—in pairs*
Standing and remaining inside a 10 yard square A pulls the ball onto his head so that it rebounds to B, standing 3 or 4 yards away, who fields or catches the ball (fig. 21).

Score: 7 out of 10.

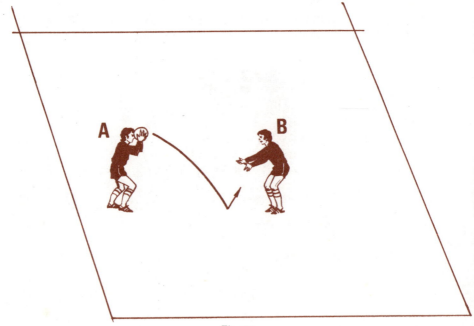

Fig. 21

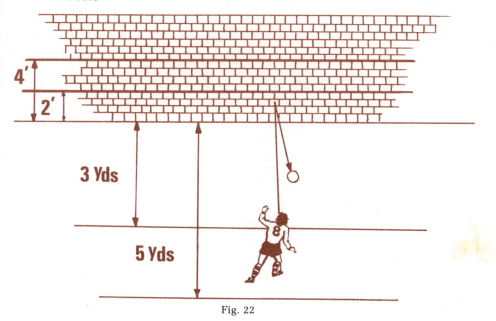

Fig. 22

3. Passing—wall and ground marks

Make marks along a wall 2 feet and 4 feet above the ground. Make two marks along the ground 3 yards and 5 yards from the ball and parallel with it (fig. 22)

From behind the 3 yard mark, pass the ball against the wall so that it always strikes the wall below the 2 foot wall mark. Each pass must be made using only three touches of the ball, or fewer if you wish.

Score: 5 in succession.

Alternative Passing Test 3. In threes, A and B stand together with feet apart facing C who stands behind a mark 3 yards from A and B.

A or B pass the ball to C who, using no more than three touches, passes the ball back to A or B who stops the ball. C's pass must arrive at A or B below knee height (fig. 23).

Score: 5 in succession.

4. Controlling and trapping

Facing the wall and remaining behind the 3 yard mark, throw the ball against the wall (fig. 24). Without using any part of your hands or arms stop the ball from bouncing past you.

Score: 5 out of 10 tries.

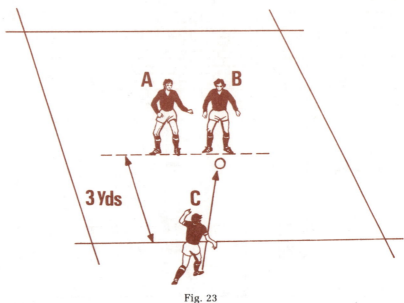

Fig. 23

Alternative Controlling and Trapping Test 4. In pairs and standing no less than 3 yards apart. Using a two-handed underhand throw, A throws the ball gently towards B who must stop it from passing him

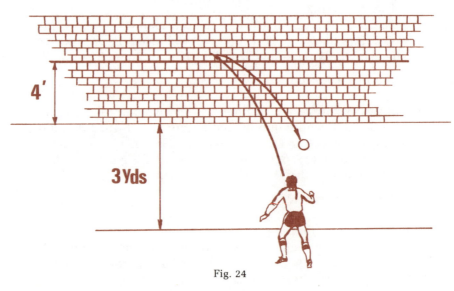

Fig. 24

by using any part of the body EXCEPT hands or arms (fig 25).

Score: 5 out of 10 tries.

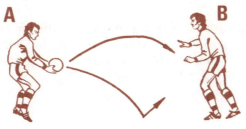

Fig. 25

5. *Dribbling*

Dribble the ball down a channel which is three grid squares long and one square wide (30 yards × 10 yards). Turn round at the post at the end of the channel and return to the starting point. Up to the turn and after it, the ball must remain within the two side lines of the channel (fig. 26).

Score: 3 successful runs.

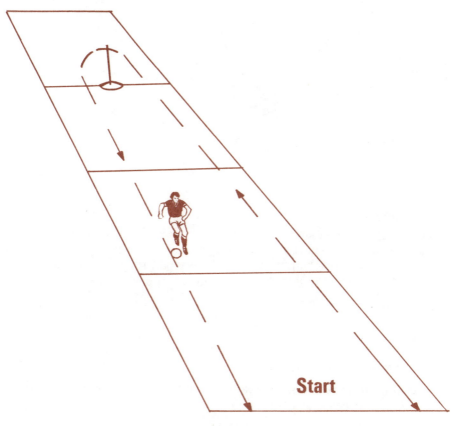

Start

Fig. 26

6. *Kicking*

In pairs A and B both stand in a grid square with one empty square between them. Kick the ball to your partner so that it doesn't touch the ground in the square which is empty. Your partner must not leave his square to collect the kicked pass (fig. 27).

  Score: 5 out of 10 tries.

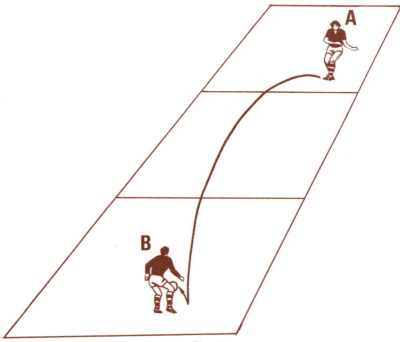

Fig. 27

7. *Shooting*

Working over 4 squares on the grid (40 yards × 10 yards), A tries to shoot through the goal 16 feet wide and 4 or 5 feet high (use corner flag posts for uprights), using a stationary ball from any position in the end square. B repeats the test from the opposite end (fig. 28).

  Score: 5 out of 10 tries.

Unit 6

Introductory Activity (5 minutes)

Working in fours across 2 squares using the mid-line as a net, two a-side tennis (see fig. 19).

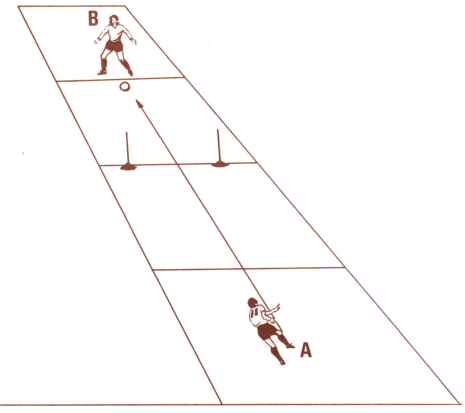

Fig. 28

The players try to build up a long sequence of passes over the net. The ball is allowed to bounce no more than twice on the ground before being returned over the net. The hand or arm may not be used to play the ball. Players on the same side of the net, if they wish, can play the ball to each other before sending it across the net. These passes do not count towards the rally.

Class Activities (20 minutes)

1. Half the class, using the coaching grid, work in fours along 4 squares (*see* fig. 28).

A goal is placed along the mid-line using 4 feet or 5 feet posts in bases, 16 feet apart.

Using a stationary ball, A and C (for example) practise shooting through the goal to score. B and D repeat the practice from the other end.

2. The remaining half of the class, with one ball each, practise juggling the ball—keeping it in the air for as many bounces as possible without allowing the ball to fall to the ground. Players may not use their hands or arms.

Group Practices—Green Star Super Skill Tests (20 minutes)

1. Touch Test—juggling
Standing and remaining inside a 10 yard square throw the ball into the air. Allow it to bounce on the ground and use any part of your body, including your hand or arm, to start a bouncing sequence going. After using your hand or arm once you must use a different part of your body for the next bounce.

Score: 6 bounces in succession.

2. Heading—in pairs
Standing and remaining inside a 10 yard square, A pulls the ball onto his head so that it rebounds to B, standing 3 or 4 yards away, who fields or catches the ball (*see* fig. 21).

Score: 7 out of 10.

3. Passing—wall and ground marks
Make marks along a wall 2 feet and 4 feet above the ground. Make two marks along the ground 3 yards and 5 yards from the wall and parallel with it (*see* fig. 22).

From behind the 3 yard mark, pass the ball against the wall so that it always strikes the wall below the 2 foot wall mark. Each pass must be made using only three touches of the ball, or fewer if you wish.

Score: 5 in succession.

Alternative Passing Test 3. In threes, A and B stand together with feet apart facing C who stands behind a mark 3 yards from A and B.

A or B pass the ball to C who, using no more than three touches, passes the ball back to A or B who stops the ball. C's pass must arrive at A or B below knee height (*see* fig. 23).

Score: 5 in succession.

4. *Controlling and trapping*

Facing the wall and remaining behind the 3 yard mark, throw the ball against the wall. Without using any part of your hands or arms stop the ball from bouncing past you (*see* fig. 24).

Score: 5 out of 10 tries.

Alternative Controlling and Trapping Test 4. In pairs and standing no less than 3 yards apart. Using a two handed underhand throw, A throws the ball gently towards B who must stop it from passing him by using any part of the body EXCEPT hands or arms (*see* fig. 25).

Score: 5 out of 10 tries.

5. *Dribbling*

Dribble the ball down a channel which is three grid squares long and one square wide (30 yards × 10 yards). Turn round at the post at the end of the channel and return to the starting point. Up to the turn and after it, the ball must remain within the two side lines of the channel (*see* fig. 26).

Score: 3 successful runs.

6. *Kicking*

In pairs A and B both stand in a grid square with one empty square between them. Kick the ball to your partner so that it doesn't touch the ground in the square which is empty. Your partner must not leave his square to collect the kicked pass (*see* fig. 27).

Score: 5 out of 10 tries.

7. *Shooting*

Working over 4 squares on the grid (40 yards × 10 yards), A tries to shoot through the goal 16 feet wide and 4 or 5 feet high (use corner flag posts for uprights), using a stationary ball from any position in the end square. B repeats the test from the opposite end (*see* fig. 28).

Score: 5 out of 10 tries.

Unit 7

Green Star Super Skill Tests

1. *Touch Test—juggling*

Standing and remaining inside a 10 yard square throw the ball into the air. Allow it to bounce on the ground and use any part of your body including your hand or arm, to start a bouncing sequence going. After using your hand or arm once you must use a different part of your body for the next bounce.

Score: 6 bounces in succession.

2. Heading—in pairs.
Standing and remaining inside a 10 yard square A pulls the ball onto his head so that it rebounds to B, standing 3 or 4 yards away, who fields or catches the ball.

Score: 7 out of 10.

3. Passing—wall and ground marks
Make marks along a wall 2 feet and 4 feet above the ground. Make two marks along the ground 3 yards and 5 yards from the wall and parallel with it.

From behind the 3 yard mark pass the ball against the wall so that it always strikes the wall below the 2 feet wall mark. Each pass must be made using only three touches of the ball, or fewer if you can.

Score: 5 in succession.

Alternative Passing Test 3. In threes, A and B stand together with feet apart facing C who stands behind a mark 3 yards from A and B.

A or B pass the ball to C who, using no more than three touches, passes the ball back to A or B who stops it. C's pass must arrive at A or B below knee height.

Score: 5 in succession.

4. Controlling and trapping
Facing the wall and remaining behind the 3 yard mark, throw the ball against the wall. Without using any part of your hands or arms stop the ball from bouncing past you.

Score: 5 out of 10 tries.

Alternative Controlling and Trapping Test 4. In pairs and standing no less than 3 yards apart. Using a two-handed underhand throw, A throws the ball gently towards B who must stop the ball from passing him by using any part of the body EXCEPT hands or arms.

Score: 5 out of 10 tries.

5. *Dribbling*

Dribble the ball down a channel which is three grid squares long and one square wide (30 yards × 10 yards). Turn round at the post at the end of the channel and return to the starting point. Up to the turn and after it, the ball must remain within the two side lines of the channel.

Score: 3 successful runs.

6. *Kicking*

In pairs A and B each stand in a grid square with one empty square between them. Kick the ball to your partner so that it doesn't touch the ground in the square which is empty. Your partner must not leave his square to collect the kicked pass.

Score: 5 out of 10 tries.

7. *Shooting*

Working over 4 squares on the grid (40 yards × 10 yards), A tries to shoot through the goal 16 feet wide and 4 or 5 feet high (use corner flag posts for uprights), using a stationary ball from any position in the end square. B repeats the test from the opposite end.

Score: 5 out of 10 tries.

V

9–10 Years

Unit 1

Introductory Activity

One ball to each player, remaining in your own square, keep the ball in the air using any part of your body below your waist—feet, knees, thighs only to do so. Your hands or arms cannot be used. You may let the ball bounce no more than twice on the ground between each contact with your foot, knee or thigh.

Practise the following points:

Position yourself close to where the ball will bounce and prepare to balance quickly on one foot so that you can play the ball with the other.

Play the ball firmly but not hurriedly.

Keep your attention on the exact point where your foot, knee or thigh will strike the ball.

Class Activity

In 3's—throw, head, catch.

Working in one square and moving freely around the square, A throws to B who, while moving, heads to C so that he can catch the ball. C throws to A or B and the throw, head, catch sequence is continued. Set a target number of consecutive sequences.

44

Remember:

when heading, turn your forehead to receive and direct the ball, by nodding it, to the third player
when you are the receiver try to anticipate, from the heading player's position and movement, the probable direction of his header.

Group Practices—Green Star Super Skill Tests

1. Touch Test—juggling
Standing and remaining inside a 10 yard square throw the ball into the air. Allow it to bounce on the ground and use any part of your body including your hand or arm, to start a bouncing sequence going. After using your hand or arm once you must use a different part of your body for the next bounce.

Score: 6 bounces in succession.

2. Heading—in pairs.
Standing and remaining inside a 10 yard square, A pulls the ball onto his head so that it rebounds to B, standing 3 or 4 yards away, who fields or catches the ball.

Score: 7 out of 10.

3. Passing—wall and ground marks
Make marks along a wall 2 feet and 4 feet above the ground. Make two marks along the ground 3 yards and 5 yards from the wall and parallel with it.

From behind the 3 yard mark pass the ball against the wall so that it always strikes the wall below the 2 feet wall mark. Each pass must be made using only three touches of the ball, or fewer if you wish.

Score: 5 in succession.

Alternative Passing Test 3. In threes, A and B stand together with feet apart facing C who stands behind a mark 3 yards from A and B.

A or B pass the ball to C who, using no more than three touches, passes the ball back to A or B who stops the ball. C's pass must arrive at A or B below knee height.

Score: 5 in succession.

4. Controlling and trapping
Facing the wall and remaining behind the 3 yard mark, throw the

ball against the wall. Without using any part of your hands or arms stop the ball from bouncing past you.

Score: 5 out of 10 tries.

Alternative Controlling and Trapping Test 4. In pairs and standing no less than 3 yards apart. Using a two-handed underhand throw, A throws the ball gently towards B who must stop the ball from passing him by using any part of the body EXCEPT hands or arms.

Score: 5 out of 10 tries.

5. Dribbling

Dribble the ball down a channel which is three grid squares long and one square wide (30 yards × 10 yards). Turn round at the post at the end of the channel and return to the starting point. Up to the turn and after it, the ball must remain within the two side lines of the channel.

Score: 3 successful runs.

6. Kicking

In pairs A and B each stand in a grid square with one empty square between them. Kick the ball to your partner so that it doesn't touch the ground in the square which is empty. Your partner must not leave his square to collect the kicked pass.

Score: 5 out of 10 tries.

7. Shooting

Working over 4 squares on the grid (40 yards × 10 yards), A tries to shoot through the goal 16 feet wide and 4 or 5 feet high (use corner flag posts for uprights), using a stationary ball from any position in the end square. B repeats the test from the opposite end.

Score: 5 out of 10 tries.

Final activity

One ball to each player, keep the ball bouncing, as in the introductory activities. On the whistle stop the ball at your feet and stand still, with your foot on the ball, as quickly as possible.

Unit 2

Introductory Activity

In pairs, in one square, one ball between two, build up a juggling rally as follows:

A throws to B (underhand throw). B may allow the ball to bounce once before playing the ball into the air using any part of his body.

Allowing no more than one further bounce on the ground B plays the ball back to A—the sequence is continued. The players try to build up a succession of passing and juggling sequences.

Practise the following points:

take up position to receive the ball early—be prepared to balance on one foot quickly
play the ball firmly not hurriedly
concentrate on an accurate contact with the ball.

Class Activities

1. In 4's working along two squares, one ball between two, the players play the ball accurately from one to the other trying to spin the ball while maintaining accuracy of passing.

Technique for spins:

Imagine a mid line vertically through the ball. When the ball is struck across and to the right of this line the ball will spin anti-clockwise (as viewed from above). If the ball is kicked in the air with this kind of spin, the ball will tend to swerve through the air from the kicker's right to his left. The opposite, of course, holds true for a ball struck on the left side of the vertical line.

Fig. 29 shows inside of right foot contact.
Fig. 30 shows outside of left foot contact.

In fig. 30, the outside of the left foot has been used to strike across the front of the ball and to the right. This kind of kick will produce a maximum of spin and swerve and a reduced amount of forward speed (travel).

2. *Trapping the Ball.*
In 3's, working in one square, A makes a ground pass to B who traps the ball with the sole of his foot (fig. 31). B pushes the ball away and

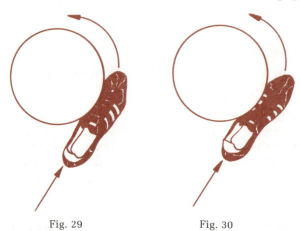

Fig. 29   Fig. 30

passes to C. The sequence is repeated round the group. A skilful player will use one touch to trap the ball, one to push it into a passing position and one to pass it.

Practise the following points:

As the ball approaches position yourself so that the ball rolls towards your trapping foot—move to balance easily and early on your other foot.

Raise the sole of your foot to receive the ball and allow the ball to come into the 'trap' made between your foot and the ground.

If the ball has been struck hard allow your foot to give with the ball slightly.

Group Practices

Separate groups can practise the following activities:

1. In 3's working along three squares, practise lofted kicking. In fig. 32, A rolls a ground pass gently to B, B kicks to C so that the ball clears the whole of A's centre square in passing. C controls the ball, passes to A who return passes so that C can kick to B and so on.

To improve your techniques:

swing your foot through the ball using a long leg
swing your foot through a point well below the horizontal mid-line of the ball

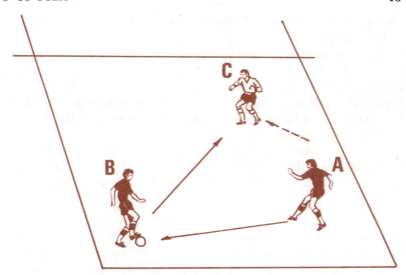

Fig. 31

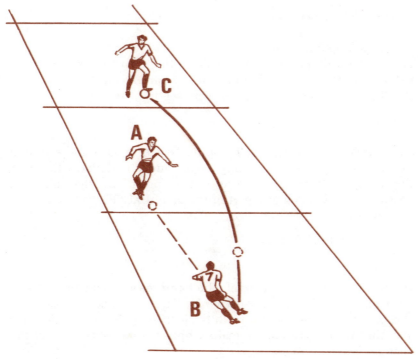

Fig. 32

swing your foot under and through the ball along an imaginary line to the target player C.

2. In 3's in one square practise throw, head, catch sequences.

3. *Passing—wall and ground marks*
Make marks along a wall 2 feet and 4 feet above the ground. Make two marks along the ground 3 yards and 5 yards from the wall and parallel with it (*see* fig. 22).

From behind the 3 yard mark pass the ball against the wall so that it always strikes the wall below the 2 feet wall mark. Each pass must be made using only three touches of the ball, or fewer if you wish.

Score: 10 in succession.

Alternative Passing Test 3. In threes, A and B stand together with feet apart facing C who stands behind a mark 3 yards from A and B.

A or B passes the ball to C who, using no more than three touches, passes the ball back to A or B who stops the ball. C's pass must arrive at A or B below knee height (*see* fig. 23).

Score: 5 in succession.

4. *Controlling and trapping*
Facing the wall and remaining behind the 3 yard mark, throw the ball against the wall. Without using any part of your hands or arms stop the ball from bouncing past you (*see* fig. 24).

Score: 5 out of 10 tries.

Alternative Controlling and Trapping Test 4. In pairs and standing no less than 3 yards apart. Using a two handed underhand throw, A throws the ball gently towards B who must stop the ball from passing him by using any part of the body EXCEPT hands or arms (*see* fig. 25).

Score: 5 out of 10 tries.

5. *Dribbling*
Dribble the ball down a channel which is three grid squares long and one square wide (30 yards × 10 yards). Turn round at the post at the end of the channel and return to the starting point. Up to the turn and after it, the ball must remain within the two side lines of the channel (*see* fig. 26).

Score: 3 successful runs.

6. *Kicking*

In pairs A and B each stand in a grid square with one empty square between them. Kick the ball to your partner so that it doesn't touch the ground in the square which is empty. Your partner must not leave his square to collect the kicked pass (see fig. 27).

Score: 5 out of 10 tries.

7. *Shooting*

Working over 4 squares on the grid (40 yards × 10 yards), A tries to shoot through the goal 16 feet wide and 4 or 5 feet high (use corner flag posts for uprights), using a stationary ball from any position in the end square. B repeats the test from the opposite end (see fig. 28).

Score: 5 out of 10 tries.

Final Activities

One ball to each player, practise free running around the grid. Find different ways of stopping the ball suddenly and starting off again quickly. Try to change direction, feint and swerve when doing so.

Unit 3

Introductory Activity

In pairs, one ball between two, in one square, build up a long rally by heading the ball from one to the other. Establish records for heading rallies or set standards such as 5, 10, 15 or 20 consecutive headers in pairs.

Class Activities

In 3's working in one square. In fig. 33, using a correct throw in technique, A throws to B who controls the ball. A and B then try to interpass against C, remaining in the square all the time, to make 3, 4 or 5 successive passes. C can only enter the square to challenge for the ball after B has touched it for the first time. A and B can position themselves as far from C as they wish.

Note the following technique:

when trapping or controlling the ball the ability to balance comfortably on one foot is vital. Receive the ball with a soft (relaxed) surface. Give with the ball to cushion its impact.

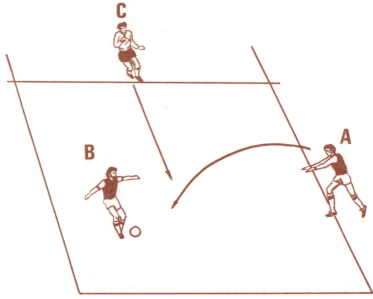

Fig. 33

Group Practices

Separate groups can practise the following activities:

1. In 3's, lofted kicking (fig. 32).
2. In 3's, throw, head, catch (see 9–10 years, Unit 1).
3. In pairs, working in two squares, A tries to spin and swerve the ball to his partner (fig. 34).
4. In pairs, pass and trap (using the sole of the foot) (fig. 31). Try using the same technique to trap a low bouncing ball.
5. Working in two squares, two versus one or three versus one, play Keep Ball. Try to build up an unbroken sequence of passes practising the following techniques.

Pass and move to a position in which you can receive a pass with the least chance of your opponent intercepting it.

Pass so that the player receiving the ball has no problem in controlling it.
6. Working in 2 squares, one versus one, A and B dribble against each other and shoot to hit the skittles (fig. 35). +3 points for a successful shot, −1 point for a miss.

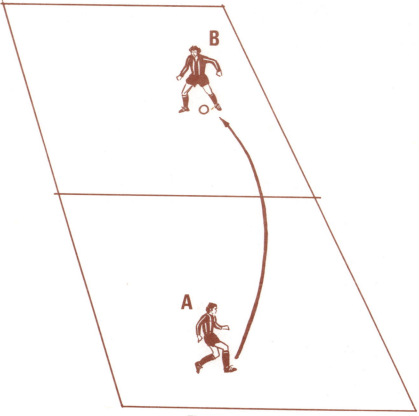

Fig. 34

Final Activities

One ball to each player, free running with the ball anywhere in the grid. Find different ways of pretending to move in one direction and turning quickly in another direction. On a signal (whistle) stop instantly with your foot on the ball.

Unit 4

Group Practices

As a change the class will go immediately into Group Practices and the lesson will follow this pattern for the rest of the unit of work.

Six activities are suggested for separate groups:

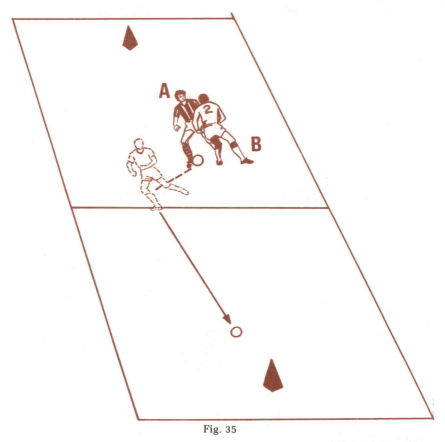

Fig. 35

1. *Skittle Soccer*. 2 versus 2 on a two or three square pitch (fig. 36).
Place the skittles in a circle 2 yards in diameter. The skittle circles
are placed 2 or 3 yards in from the end-lines and play can proceed
around and behind them. If the ball goes out of play it is rolled back
into play. A goal is scored whenever the ball or a defending player
knocks the skittle down.

The following techniques are useful in this game:

When your partner has the ball try to get into positions so that if he
passes behind one or both opponents you can reach the ball before
they do.
    When your opponents have the ball defend so that an opponent
can never take a clear shot at goal. Try also to prevent an opponent
from passing the ball behind you to his team mate who may be able
to shoot.

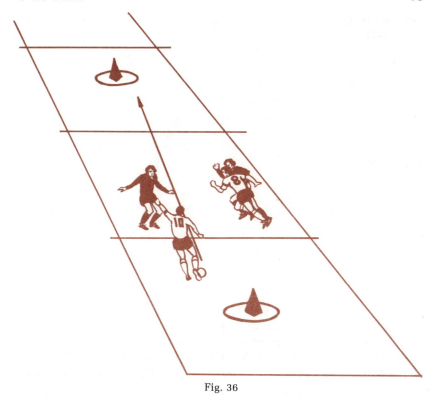

Fig. 36

2. *Soccer Throw In—Control—Pass.* In 3's, using two squares, A throws in to B, using a correct throw in. Both feet must be on or behind the line and the ball must be delivered from over the head using two hands. B controls and passes to C using no more than three (or two) touches to do so. Change the group round. (See 9–10 years, Unit 3).

Note the techniques for throwing and receiving.

Thrower—the ball must be thrown so that the receiver can stop it with his foot easily without stretching to do so, or so that he can catch it (control it) on his body easily.

Receiver—look for a target player before the ball arrives. As the ball is drawn back over the thrower's head move quickly into position and slow down or stop as the ball is thrown to you.

3. *Spinning Kick.* In pairs, A tries to spin and swerve his kick along

the two square pitch to B, either on the ground or through the air. (*See* 9–10 years, Unit 2).

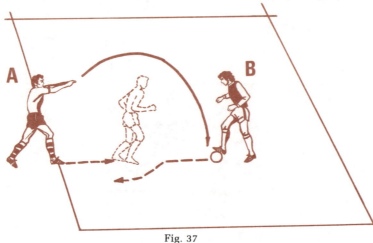

Fig. 37

4. *Throw, Trap and Dribble.* In pairs, in fig. 37, A throws in to B who traps the ball under the sole of his foot. As soon as B has made his first contact with the ball A can move to challenge him. B will try to control and dribble the ball over the end line behind A. Change over. Practise techniques described in Unit 3, 9–10 years.

5. In 2 squares, 2 versus 1 or 3 versus 1 practise Keep Ball. Set target scores of successive passes—5, 10, 15 and so on.

6. 1 versus 1 in 2 squares, dribble and shoot. (*See* Group Practices 9–10 years, Unit 3).

Class Activities

In groups of 6, pick 3 teams of 2. Use skittles, cones or posts to make a goal 10 yards (30 feet) wide, one team of 2 becomes the goalkeepers. The remaining two teams play against each other to score. The first team to score 3 goals causes its opponents to go into goal. The goalkeeping team comes out and the game continues.

The goals are best located so that if a shot misses (or scores), the ball cannot roll too far away. A fixed (marked) playing pitch is not needed. Players will confine their play to an area near to goal. After a goal, an unsuccessful shot or a save, one of the goalkeepers lobs the ball gently beyond all the players so that the game can continue (fig. 38).

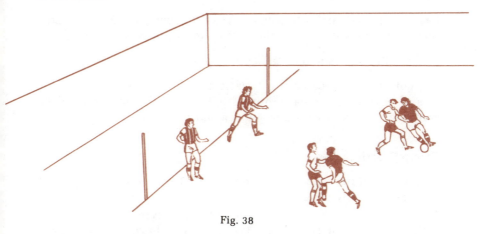

Fig. 38

Remember the following points when shooting:

Since 6 players will be in a relatively small area in front of goal for most of the time, SHOOT as soon as you can see a line from your foot through the ball to goal. ALWAYS place the ball to beat the goalkeepers. NEVER try to hit the ball as hard as possible, as if trying to break it.

Unit 5

Introductory Activities

In 4's, in one square, play the ball freely among the four and keep the ball inside the square all the time. Build up record breaking or target sequences of volley rallies. A volley is when the ball is passed while in the air. The ball is allowed to bounce only once on the ground in between each volley. The technique is described below.

Volleying the ball, like trapping, depends upon your ability to balance easily and quickly on one foot so that you can play the ball with the other.

When striking the ball play it upwards towards your team mate. Strike it firmly but gently.

Look at the ball not where you expect it to go.

Class Activities

Skittle ball, 2 v 2, using hands only (fig. 36). The ball is caught and passed using one or both hands to do so. To score, a player may drop the ball and kick it to knock the skittles down OR throw them down.

The following is good goalkeeping practice:

Use both hands to catch high passes so that your hands are to the side of or behind the ball; thumbs point towards each other. Keep your head still and your eyes on the ball when jumping to catch.

Group Practices

1. 2 v 1 in one square, play Keep Ball to try for set targets of unbroken passing sequences.
2. Two teams of 3 play around and outside a circle of 5 yards radius with a skittle in the centre (fig. 39). A, B and C have five attempts to

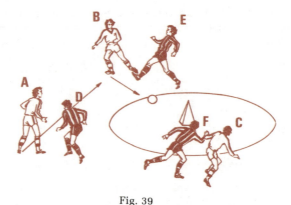

Fig. 39

score. D, E and F defend the skittle. A shot which misses counts as a goal to the defending team. The first team to score 3 goals wins and the teams change over.

Techniques for shooting practice:

As in all shooting situations if you think there is an unblocked line from your foot, through the ball to the target (goal), shoot!

Build up your approach play carefully and if necessary slowly. To get a shot in pass to a team-mate (or dribble) past an opponent quickly and shoot early.

3. In pairs in one square, A starts in one corner with the ball and

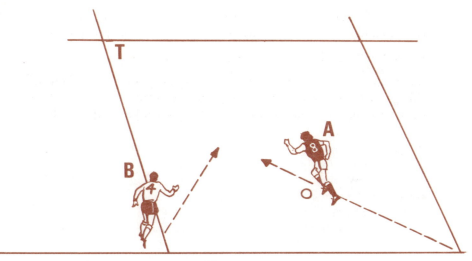

Fig. 40

attacks an agreed target corner T by dribbling past B. B must start in a neutral corner and remain there until A dribbles out of his corner (fig. 40).

To score, A must enter the target corner and put one foot on the ball when stopping it.

4. *Soccer throw-in competition for distance.* All throws are measured and recorded. Group, class and school records may be established.

Practise the following techniques:

Throw from a position which allows you to bend your body a long way back before releasing the ball powerfully forward WITHOUT lifting one or both feet from the ground. Distance is obtained from a combination of height and power. Too much height and you waste power. Too much power and you rarely get enough height. In both cases distance suffers.

5. *Ground passing—instant target.* In pairs, practising in two squares, A and B run freely around their respective squares, A with the ball and B without. When he chooses to do so, B stands still with feet apart. As soon as B presents this target position A has two (one) touches to pass the ball along the ground through the target made by B's feet.

Note the points below:

Try to divide your attention between close ball control and the target player.

The first of your two touches must be used to set the ball up (position it) so that your second touch can be used to pass it through the target.

Look at the ball when you strike it NOT at the target.

6. *Long kicking.* See Group Practices 9–10 years, Unit 2, and practise ways of spinning the ball.

Try to strike the ball under its fattest part so that the ball rises very steeply to pass over the empty square. How much back spin can you put on the ball?

Can you kick the ball to your partner to make it lift and swerve?

Unit 6

Class Activities

3 v 3 competition matches played on a 30 yard × 20 yard or a 30 yard × 30 yard pitch.

Each match lasts for 4 minutes.

The class is divided into 6–8 teams and each team plays every other team once. The teams must be selected to make competition as even as possible.

The three player unit or triangle, in many ways, is the basis for all football ideas. Use the 3 v 3 games to teach this idea.

In fig. 41, where player A has the room to pass to either B or C the triangle formed is helpful to him.

In fig. 42, where the opponent D has made a choice of pass more difficult for A, C has helped by moving forward to show himself for a pass. A can now pass forwards or sideways.

Group Practices—Red Star Super Skill Tests

1. *Touch Test—juggling*
In pairs, in a 10 yard square, each player must play the ball alternately and he can use any part of his body **except his hand or arm,** to keep the sequence going. The ball may be allowed to bounce on the ground once only as it is passed from one player to another.

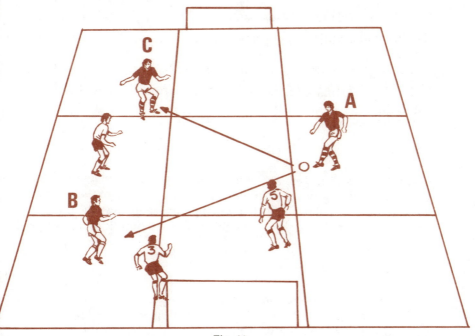

Fig. 41

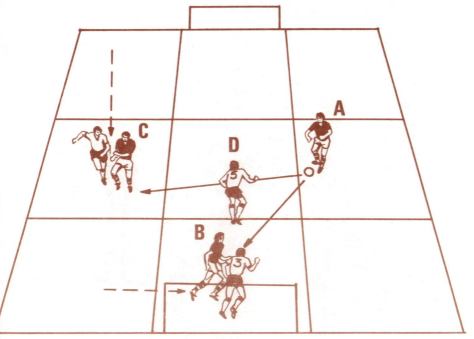

Fig. 42

Both players and the ball must remain inside the square all the time.

Score: 7 bounces in succession.

2. *Heading*
From behind the mark on the ground 3 yards from the wall, head the ball to hit the wall above the 4 foot mark. Catch the return before it touches the ground.

Score: 5 consecutive headers.

Alternative Heading Test 2. Where a wall is not available: in threes, standing about 2 yards apart in line, A heads the ball over the middle player to the third player. The ball must pass cleanly over the middle player and must be caught by the third player before it touches the ground (fig. 43).

Score: 5 consecutive headers.

3. *Passing—wall and ground marks*
From behind the mark 5 yards from the wall, pass the ball so that it strikes the wall below the wall mark 2 feet high. Use your left and right feet alternately. Each pass must be made using two touches, or fewer if you wish. (See Green Star Tests).

Score: 10 in succession.

Fig. 43

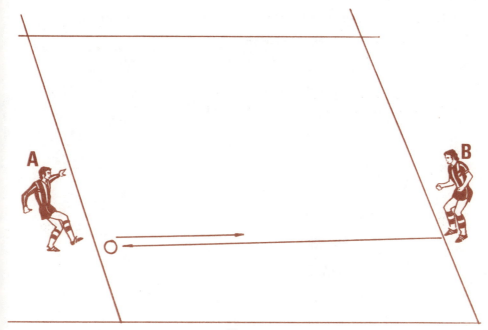

Fig. 44

Alternative Passing Test 3. In threes, A and B stand together with feet apart facing C who stands behind a mark 5 yards away. A or B rolls the ball to C who must return the ball with a pass using two touches only, or fewer. The return passes from A must be made using your left and right feet alternately (fig. 23).

Score: 10 in succession.

4. *Controlling and trapping*
In pairs, standing outside and playing across a 10 yard grid square, A passes to B who must stop the ball with one touch and return the ball to his partner using a second touch only. Each player is allowed only two touches (fig. 44).

Score: 8 (total) in succession.

5. *Dribbling*
Place 4 skittles at the corners of a 10 yard grid square. Dribble the

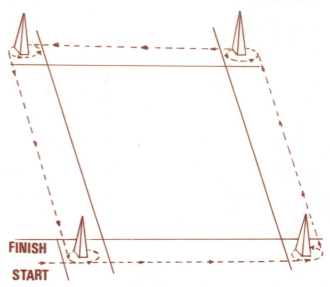

Fig. 45

Fig. 46

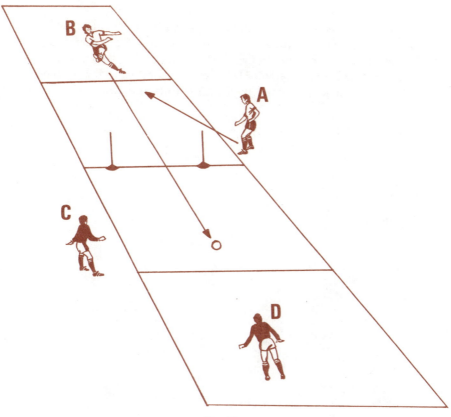

Fig. 47

ball round the square. At each corner dribble the ball completely round the skittle before going on to the next. Make 2 trips—the second must be in the opposite direction to the first (fig. 45).

Score: 2 successful runs.

6. *Kicking*

A and B each stand in a grid square with two empty squares between them. The players kick the ball to each other so that it clears the two empty squares. When receiving the ball a player must not leave his square to collect the pass (fig. 46).

Score: 5 out of 10 tries.

7. *Shooting*
In fours, using 4 squares on the grid (40 yards × 10 yards) and from outside the grid, A rolls a ground pass into B's square. B runs forward to shoot through the goal. He must do so in two touches, one to control and one to shoot. He may shoot first time if he wishes.

The sequence is repeated by C and D from the other end (fig. 47) (see page 65).

Score: 5 out of 10 tries.

Unit 7

As for Unit 6.

VI

10–11 Years

Unit 1

Introductory and Class Activities

3 v 3 matches and tournament. (*See* 9–10 Years. Unit 6).
Having shown the need for the triangle pattern and the importance of supporting (helping) positions in attacking play, the next priority is to show how players can interchange positions to get away from close marking opponents while maintaining sensible supporting positions.

In fig. 48. A cannot pass to B or C easily. They are closely marked. A himself will soon be under challenge from D.

In fig 49. C has moved behind A into a safe supporting position. Should the nearest opponent follow him or not? B has moved across field into the position left by C. The resulting situation is that A can attack opponent D, particularly through the shaded space. If he doesn't, A and B can still play for attacking positions against opponents D and E.

Making space for other players by drawing or tempting opponents into parts of the pitch where they don't really want to go is an important soccer skill.

Group Practices—Red Star Super Skill Tests

1. *Touch Test—juggling*
In pairs, in a 10 yard square, each player must play the ball

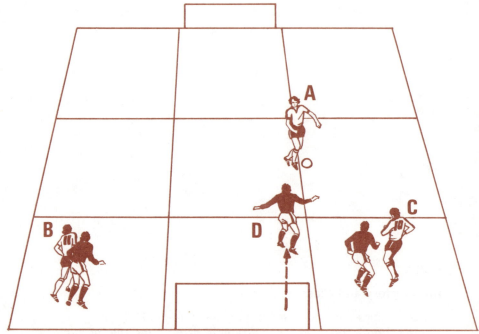

Fig. 48

alternately and he can use any part of his body **except his hand or arm,** to keep the sequence going. The ball may be allowed to bounce on the ground once only as it is passed from one player to another. Both players and the ball must remain inside the square all the time.

Score: 7 bounces in succession.

2. *Heading*
From behind the mark on the ground 3 yards from the wall, head the ball to hit the wall above the 4 foot mark. Catch the return before it touches the ground.

Score: 5 consecutive headers.

Alternative Heading Test 2. Where a wall is not available: in threes, standing about 2 yards apart in line, A heads the ball over the middle player to the third player. The ball must pass cleanly over the middle player and must be caught by the third player before it touches the ground (fig. 43).

Score: 5 consecutive headers.

3. Passing—wall and ground marks

From behind the mark 5 yards from the wall, pass the ball so that it strikes the wall below the wall mark 2 feet high. Use your left and right feet alternately. Each pass must be made using two touches, or fewer if you wish. (*see* Green Star Tests).

Score: 10 in succession.

Alternative Passing Test 3. In threes, A and B stand together with feet apart facing C who stands behind a mark 5 yards away. A or B rolls the ball to C who must return the ball with a pass using two touches only, or fewer. The return passes from A must be made using your left and right feet alternately.

Score: 10 in succession.

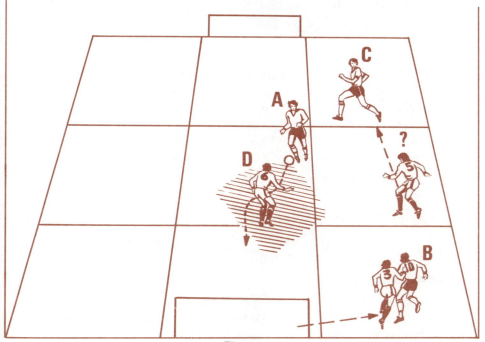

Fig. 49

4. *Controlling and trapping*
In pairs, standing outside and playing across a 10 yard grid square, A passes to B who must stop the ball with one touch and return the ball to his partner using a second touch only. Each player is allowed only two touches (fig. 44).

Score: 8 (total) in succession.

5. *Dribbling*
Place 4 skittles at the corners of a 10 yard grid square. Dribble the ball round the square. At each corner dribble the ball completely round the skittle before going on to the next. Make 2 trips—the second must be in the opposite direction to the first (fig. 45).

Score: 2 successful runs.

6. *Kicking*
A and B each stand in a grid square with two empty squares between them. The players kick the ball to each other so that it clears the two empty squares. When receiving the ball a player must not leave his square to collect the pass (fig. 46).

Score: 5 out of 10 tries.

7. *Shooting*
In fours, using 4 squares on the grid (40 yards × 10 yards) and from outside the grid, A rolls a ground pass into B's square. B runs forward to shoot through the goal. He must do so in two touches, one to control and one to shoot. He may shoot first time if he wishes.

The sequence is repeated by C and D from the other end (fig. 47) (see page 65).

Score: 5 out of 10 tries.

Unit 2

Introductory Activity

In pairs, working in one square with one ball. Using two hands, A throws underhand to B who plays the ball back while it is in the air. A then tries to give a FIRST TIME return pass to B who catches the ball and repeats the sequence.

Practise techniques for short volley passing:

In short volley passing the foot is swung from a knee movement rather than a hip movement.

Try to push your foot through the ball, firmly but with half force, towards the target.

Use the broad inside part of your foot and ankle or your instep (the tops of your toes and the laces of your shoes).

Class Activity

In 3's, in one square, using one ball (fig. 50). The player with the ball can choose to play the ball into the empty corner OR to either of the other two players. The players off the ball (those not in possession of it) must change their corners.

Early in the practice insist that the players touch the ball *twice* before passing. Later the players must judge the strength of the pass when playing it first time.

Group Practices

1. In one square, in threes, A throws to B who has three (two) touches in which to control and pass to C. The target player (the player receiving the pass) can move around the square, as the ball is

Fig. 50

being thrown, before stopping to show himself as a target.

Note the following points:

Make your controlling surface as soft as possible. Give with the ball so that you almost catch the ball on or under the controlling surface.

2. In pairs, working across and outside one square, A passes to B and then moves to change position along the line. B in two (or one) touches tries to play a good ground pass to A's feet (fig. 51).

Several points should be borne in mind for ball control:

When B has anticipated the line of A's pass he should glance up to note A's new position.

Control the ball in a direction which makes a pass towards the target player easy.

Fig. 51

Concentrate on precise, accurate contacts with the ball when controlling and when passing.

3. In pairs, football throw in competition for distance and accuracy. Starting behind a mark on the ground, A throws to B who may move one foot to control the ball or he may catch it. If he is successful he moves one yard further away from A until, between them, they find the longest, accurate throw.

4. In 4.s, in two squares, play 1 v 1 Keep Ball. How many touches can you make (and count) in 2 minutes or before your opponent touches the ball or forces it off the pitch?

When dribbling the ball remember the following points:

Although the group of four is split into two pairs the players who are dribbling must be aware of all possible sources of interference.

Dribble with your head up.

If in doubt keep your opponent away from the ball by positioning your body between him and the ball.

5. Long kicking for accuracy. In pairs, using hoops on the ground as targets, players try to maintain accuracy while trying longer, lofted kicks to drop the ball first bounce in a hoop. Distances are increased by moving the hoops further away from the starting line. The group works in pairs. One kicks for the target while the other, positioned someway behind the hoop, retrieves. The retriever must use only football techniques to stop, control and return the ball.

When kicking the ball remember the techniques:

Kick with the tops of your toes or the bottom laces of your shoes.

Strike the ball below its fattest part.

Kick through the ball swinging your foot along an imaginary line to your target.

6. In 2 squares, two players a-side, using the mid-line as a net, the players try to build up a record number of passes over and across the net. The player may touch the ball ONCE ONLY before it MUST be played back in the air over the net.

Unit 3

For a change this unit of work begins with Group Practices which are followed by Class Activities.

Group Practices

1. In 3's, in one square using one ball, pass and change corners. For particular points to practise, *see* 10–11 Years, Class Activities, Unit 2.

2. 3 v 3 Skittle ball. For particular points to practise *see* 9–10 Years, Group Practices, Unit 5.

3. Dribbling Practice. Running clockwise outside the square, dribble with the foot nearest to the square all the time. Use the inside and the outside of your foot to control the ball. Change direction and use the other foot as the dribbling foot.

Practise the following techniques:

Try to run level with the ball all the time.

    Play the ball along using light taps with the inside and outside of your foot frequently.

4. In groups of 4, A throws underarm to B who tries to head the ball through the hoop held by C. C holds the hoop away from his body at different heights and D stands behind C to retrieve the ball (fig. 52).

Fig. 52

Practise the following points:

As the ball meets your forehead turn your neck to direct the ball towards the target. Nod through the ball along an imaginary line to your target.

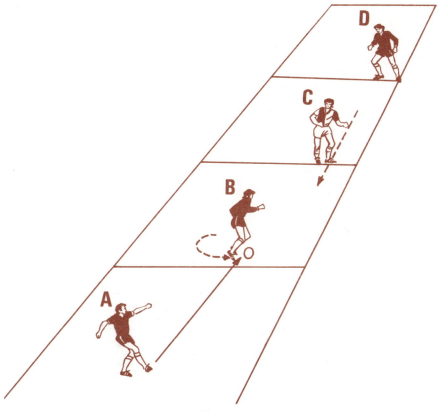

Fig. 53

5. Working in four squares, in groups of 4 (fig. 53). A plays a pass to B, standing in the middle square. As soon as the ball enters the middle square, C starting from outside it may challenge for or try to intercept the ball. On receiving the ball B turns and tries to pass to D in the far end square. Players can reverse their positions so that the practice can begin from D's end.

Passing will be improved by practising the following:

Try to receive the pass half turned towards your target player. If your opponent is still some way from you when you have turned, sight your target player's position and give a pass early. If your opponent has moved close to you as you turn pretend to pass, turn away and then pass.

6. 1 v 1, in 2 squares, target dribbling.

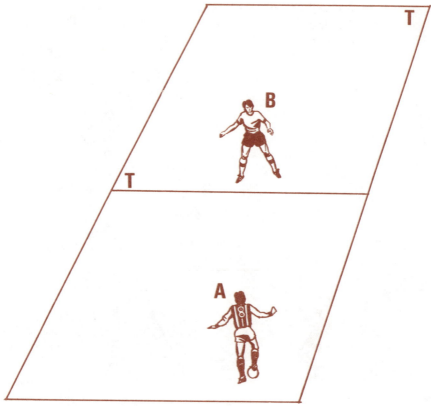

Fig. 54

There are two target corners in fig. 54. When A takes his foot off the ball, B may begin his challenge to prevent A getting into either of the T corners.

Deceive your opponent in the following ways:

Pretend (feint) to attack one T corner and turn or accelerate quickly to attack the other.

Use changes of pace to deceive your opponent.

Use your eyes to deceive him or at least don't allow them to give you away!

Class Activity

Goalkeeping. In pairs, working across a square, A throws the ball underhand (or rolls it) to B who fields it or catches it like a goalkeeper. Having gathered the ball B kicks it gently out of his hands back to his partner.

Final Activity

In 4's, working in 2 squares, A and C throw to B and D respectively using correct soccer throw in techniques. The thrower throws to his partner so that he can trap or control the ball taking no more than one step in any direction to do so.

Unit 4

Introductory Activities

Working across and outside one square, in pairs, players try to build up unbroken sequences of first time passes.

Concentrate your attention on EXACTLY where you intend to strike the ball.

Strike through the fattest part of the ball (or slightly above it) towards your target so that the ball stays on the ground.

Class Activities

In 2 squares, 4 v 2, play Keep Ball. How many uninterrupted passes can you make before the sequence is broken?

Use all the space available to give yourself time to receive a pass (and to give one).

Position yourself so that there is always a clear 'line of sight' from you to the ball.

In fig. 55 D is hidden behind his own player C and the nearby opponent but B has moved to find a clear line of sight from his position to the ball.

Group Practices

1. In 3's, in 2 squares (or 1 square), 2 v 1 throw in, control and interpass against the opponent.

Having started the practice A and B try to make a set number of uninterrupted passes against C.

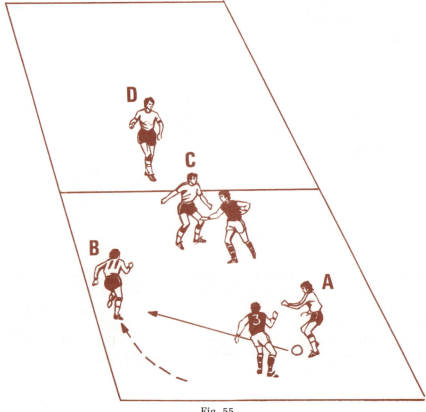

Fig. 55

A and B should practise a throw which allows B to move towards A to control the ball.

Interpassing will be successful when opponents are never allowed to get so near to the player with the ball that he cannot pass easily to a target player. Highly skilful, clever players, of course, may deliberately tempt opponents to come very close indeed before flicking a pass away.

2. In pairs, playing across and outside a square, aim for a record unbroken sequence of first time ground passes.

3. In three's, working along 4 squares. A throws to B who tries to control the ball before it touches the ground. B passes the ball back to A who then plays a pass to C in the far end square. C returns the practice, through B to A (fig. 56).

4. In 4's, working over 2 squares, 2 v 2 Skittle Soccer.

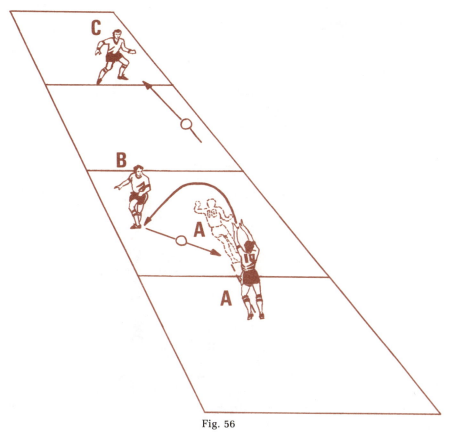

Fig. 56

5. In 2's, working over 4 squares, practise lofted kicking to drop the ball into target hoops. One player kicks while the other retrieves behind the target hoops (fig. 57).

6. In 4's working in 4 squares (20 yards × 20 yards). A rolls a ground pass to B who kicks a lofted pass across to C. C pushes a ground pass to D who kicks a lofted pass to A and so on (fig. 58).

Even though your kick will change the direction of movement of the ball, the principles are the same as for kicking a straight pass.

Kick **through** a point, below the fattest part of the ball, along its vertical mid-line, towards the target player. Swing your foot **through** this point along an imaginary line to your target.

Attend to the **exact** point at which you intend to strike the ball and avoid any tendency to look up to see the result of your kick before the kick is completed!

Fig. 57

Final Activity

Volley kicking. In 2 squares, 6 players play 5 v 1 (or 4 v 2) Volley and Catch. Volley the ball from your hands so that it can be caught by one of your team mates.

   How many passes can you build up in sequence?

Unit 5

Introductory Activity

One player with one ball builds up long juggling sequences. Challenge the players by setting different sequences, i.e. left foot, right foot counts as one, or either foot followed by a header counts as one and so on.

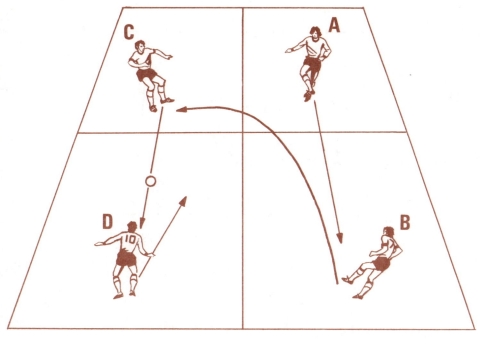

Fig. 58

Class Activities

In pairs, working across 2 squares. How long a sequence of uninterrupted volley passes can you build up using your feet only? The ball
is allowed to bounce twice in between each return volley. The ball
must be in the air as it crosses the mid-line.

Group Practices

1. 2 v 2 v 2 in 3 squares. Goals may be made using posts in bases or
skittles, 8 yards apart (fig. 59). The game is played anywhere in the
three squares. The ball can be played in any direction around or over
the goals and play is continuous. The first team to score three goals
goes into goal (alternatively the winners stay out while the losers go
in goal). Remember when shooting to concentrate on taking low
shots which hit the target.

Make sure that your body stays well over (above) the ball.

2. 3 v 3. Circle Skittle Ball.

3. Speed dribbling races over 3 or 4 squares, around obstacles if you
wish.

Fig. 59

4. Throwing for accuracy competitions. The distance should be more than 10 yards and a correct soccer throw in technique MUST be used. Hoops can be used as targets. Work in pairs, one throwing and one retrieving.

5. In 3's, working across and outside one square, two players on one side, one on the other (fig. 60). A and B are permitted to use two (or

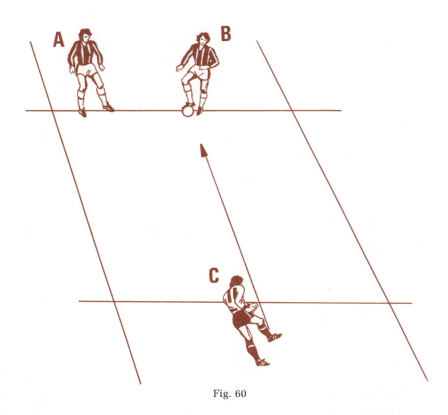

Fig. 60

three) touches to control and pass the ball to C. C must give a first time return ground pass.

Final Activity

In one square, 2 players move anywhere in the square keeping the ball in the air all the time. On a signal (whistle) one player must stop the ball and stand still with his foot on the ball as quickly as he can.

Unit 6

Class Activity

2 v 2 Skittle Soccer competition, working in 2 squares.

Group Practices—Black Star Super Skill Tests.

1. *Touch Test—juggling*
In a 10 yard square, by yourself, keep the ball in the air continuously **without** using your hand or arm. The ball must not touch the ground and you must remain inside the square all the time.

Score: 6 bounces in succession.

2. *Heading*
In threes, each player heads the ball in turn. Keep the heading sequence going without the ball touching the ground.

Score: 6 headers in succession.

3. *Passing*
In pairs, standing outside a 10 yard grid square, pass the ball across the square continuously. Make the passes using one touch only.

Score: 10 in succession.

4. *Controlling and trapping*
Starting behind the mark 5 yards from the wall, throw the ball above the 4 foot wall mark. As the ball rebounds, trap or control it using any part of either foot and, using no more than two further touches, play a ground pass against the wall and below the 2 foot mark. A maximum of 3 touches may be used to control and pass the ball.

Score: 5 in succession.

Alternative Controlling and Trapping Test 4. In threes, A and B standing together face C who stands behind a mark 5 yards away.
A or B lob the ball to C so that C can trap or control the ball using any part of either foot. Using no more than one further touch (i.e. two touches in all) C passes the ball below knee height to A or B.

Score: 5 in succession.

5. *Dribbling*

Place 4 skittles at the corners of a 10 yard square. Dribble the ball round the square. At the first skittle dribble round it using the inside of one foot only. At the second skittle use the outside of the foot only and so on, using the inside and the outside of either foot alternately during both runs.

Score: 2 successful runs.

6. *Kicking—in fours*

In fig. 61, A rolls the ball to C who controls and kicks the ball to B clearing the middle square. B, receiving the ball, must control it using any part of his body to do so in his own square. The test can be continued with B rolling the ball to D and so on (fig. 61).

Score: 5 out of 10 tries, each player.

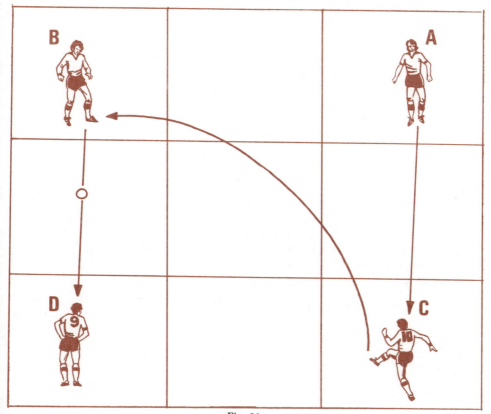

Fig. 61

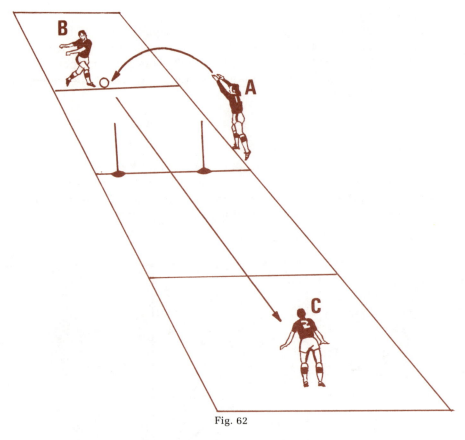

Fig. 62

7. Shooting—in threes

In fig. 62, A throws the ball so that it bounces in B's square. B, taking a shot from inside the end square, must control the ball on the first bounce or in the air and shoot accurately through the goal using not more than 3 touches to do so. C can repeat the test from the other end. A can serve for both players.

Score: 6 out of 10 tries.

Unit 7

Class Activity

4 v 4 Skittle Soccer in 4 squares.

Group Practices—Black Star Super Skill Tests

1. *Touch Test—juggling*
In a 10 yard square, by yourself, keep the ball in the air continuously **without** using your hand or arm. The ball must not touch the ground and you must remain inside the square all the time.

   Score: 6 bounces in succession.

2. *Heading*
In threes, each player heads the ball in turn. Keep the heading sequence going without the ball touching the ground.

   Score: 6 headers in succession.

3. *Passing*
In pairs, standing outside a 10 yard grid square, pass the ball across the square continuously. Make the passes using only one touch.

4. *Controlling and trapping*
Starting behind the mark 5 yards from the wall, throw the ball above the 4 foot wall mark. As the ball rebounds, trap or control the ball using any part of either foot and, using no more than two further touches, play a ground pass against the wall and below the 2 foot mark. A maximum of 3 touches may be used to control and pass the ball.

   Score: 5 in succession

Alternative Controlling and Trapping Test 4. In threes, A and B standing together face C who stands behind a mark 5 yards away.
   A or B lob the ball to C so that C can trap or control the ball using any part of either foot. Using no more than one further touch (i.e. two touches in all) C passes the ball below knee height to A or B.

   Score: 5 in succession.

5. *Dribbling*
Place 4 skittles at the corners of a 10 yard grid square. Dribble the ball round the square. At the first skittle dribble round it using the inside of one foot only. At the second skittle use the outside of the foot only and so on using the inside and the outside of either foot alternately during both runs.

   Score: 2 successful runs.

6. *Kicking—in fours*
A rolls the ball to C who controls and kicks the ball to B clearing the middle square. B, receiving the ball, must control it using any part of his body to do so in his own square. The test can be continued with B rolling the ball to D and so on.

Score: 5 out of 10 tries, each player.

7. *Shooting—in threes*
A throws the ball so that it bounces in B's square. B, taking a shot from inside the end square, must control the ball first bounce or in the air and shoot accurately through the goal using not more than 3 touches to do so. C can repeat the test from the other end.
A can serve for both players.

Score: 6 out of 10 tries.

VII

11–12 Years

Unit 1

Introductory Activity

4 v 4 Skittle Soccer on a pitch 4 squares long.

Try to draw defenders away from each other and away from their goal before making a determined attempt to get past them to shoot and score. This is called stretching a defence.

Group Practices—Black Star Super Skill Tests

1. *Touch Test—juggling*

In a 10 yard square, by yourself, keep the ball in the air continuously **without** using your hand or arm. The ball must not touch the ground and you must remain inside the square all the time.

Score: 6 bounces in succession.

2. *Heading*

In threes, each player heads the ball in turn. Keep the heading sequence going without the ball touching the ground.

Score: 6 headers in succession.

3. *Passing*
In pairs, standing outside a 10 yard grid square, pass the ball across the square continuously. Make the passes using one touch only.

   Score: 10 in succession.

4. *Controlling and trapping*
Starting behind the mark 5 yards from the wall, throw the ball above the wall mark 4 feet high. As the ball rebounds, trap or control the ball using any part of either foot and, using no more than two further touches, play a ground pass against the wall and below the 2 foot mark. A maximum of 3 touches may be used to control and pass the ball.

   Score: 5 in succession.

Alternative Controlling and Trapping Test 4. In threes, A and B standing together face C who stands behind a mark 5 yards away.
   A or B lob the ball to C so that C can trap or control the ball using any part of either foot. Using no more than one further touch (i.e. two touches in all) C passes the ball below knee height to A or B.

   Score: 5 in succession.

5. *Dribbling*
Place 4 skittles at the corners of a 10 yard grid square. Dribble the ball round the square. At the first skittle dribble round it using the inside of one foot only. At the second skittle use the outside of the foot only and so on using the inside and the outside of either foot alternately during both runs.

   Score: 2 successful runs.

6. *Kicking—in fours*
A rolls the ball to C who controls and kicks the ball to B clearing the middle square. B, receiving the ball, must control it using any part of his body to do so in his own square. The test can be continued with B rolling the ball to D and so on.

   Score: 5 out of 10 tries, each player.

7. *Shooting—in threes*
A throws the ball so that it bounces in B's square. B, taking a shot from inside the end square, must control the ball first bounce or in

the air and shoot accurately through the goal using not more than 3 touches to do so. C can repeat the test from the other end.

A can serve for both players.

Score: 6 out of 10 tries.

Unit 2

Introductory Activity

In 4's, A throws from the side to B who heads for maximum distance. C takes up position where the ball first touches the ground. D serves from the side to C who heads the ball towards B for maximum distance. A marks the distance of C's header by standing there. B from the side serves to A and so on.

When heading:

throw your head at and **through** the ball.
head the ball **upwards** and away.
use the flat front of your forehead to strike the ball.

Class Activity

In 8's, 4 v 4 on a pitch 4 squares long. Play 'Sentry Soccer', (fig. 63).

To make spaces through which the ball can be passed to players who can then pass the ball to the sentry (S1 or S2), other players MUST take up the widest positions. Sometimes it is necessary to pass backwards in order to be able to pass forwards accurately.

Group Practices

1. *Heading for distance* (see Introductory Activity).
2. *Target Shooting.*
   In 3 squares—place a skittle in each of the end squares.
   The skittles are placed, as shown in fig. 64 at the beginning of practice. As each skittle is knocked down it is moved backwards the distance of the height of the skittle. The first team to force its target skittle onto or beyond the opposite end line and hit it, wins.

Fig. 63

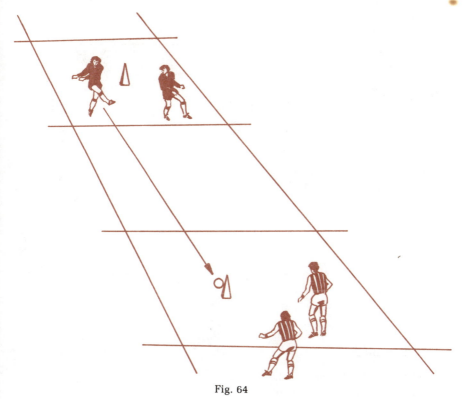

Fig. 64

Good techniques for target kicking:

Your non-kicking foot is placed close to the ball. Drive your foot through an imaginary line from the centre of the ball through the centre of the target.

Look at the ball to shoot accurately, not at the target.

3. In 2 squares—4 to a square. Throw—head—control and pass.

The group aims to produce the above sequence in the fewest possible touches and then tries to build up the largest number of one touch sequences.

4. In 4's. In fig. 65, A throws to B, C and D in turn. Each player controls the ball with at least one touch and passes the ball back to A. The players change positions until each has completed his turn as the server. The two teams compete against each other to finish in their team starting positions first.

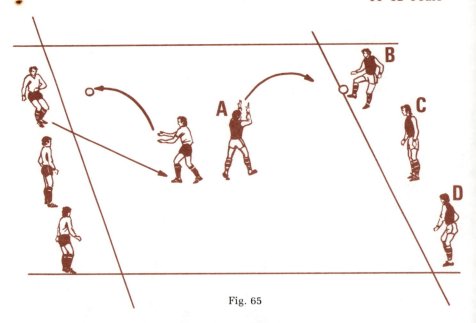

Fig. 65

5. In 4 squares. 5 v 3 play Keep Ball using one of the following special rules:

three touches or less
left foot only (or right foot)
all passes below knee height
outside of the foot passing only.

Useful techniques:

Position yourself so that there is always a clear channel for a pass from the ball to you.
    Always EXPECT the ball to come even if it seems unlikely.
6. In 4's—two teams on a pitch 4 squares long. 3 v 3 and 2 sentries. Hand ball or basketball passing is used and to score, a team interpasses until the ball can be headed into the hands of the sentry.

Final Activity

Solo juggling— keep the ball in the air as long as possible using alternately any part of your body above the waist and any part below your waist.

Unit 3

Introductory Activity

In pairs, A keeps the ball in the air for 3 bounces and then passes to his partner B who repeats the sequence and so on. The ball may bounce on the ground once only as it is transferred from A to B and from B to A. How many can you score?

Class Activity

Working across and outside 2 grid squares, practise ground passing. Each player, when receiving the ball, has not more than two touches in which to control and give a return pass to his partner.

Fig. 66

Techniques for ground passing:

Strike the ball slightly above the horizontal mid-line and swing your foot through the ball towards the target player. The resulting top spin or forward roll on the ball will help it to carry to your partner (fig. 66). In your controlling movement try to knock the ball forward slightly and outside the foot which you intend to use to give the return pass.

Group Practices

1. *Sentry Soccer.*
3 v 3 working in 3 squares. One sentry must be on each end line **all** the time. Using soccer techniques only pass the ball into your

sentry's hands to score.

Change the sentries each time a goal is scored.

Techniques for Sentry Soccer:

When you are waiting to receive the ball (and when you have it) ALWAYS look for your next pass or your next position. Always take up a standing position which will allow you to give a good first time pass, if you need to, when the ball comes.

2. Practising in pairs over two squares (fig. 67). How much can you make the ball swerve away from your partner before it swerves back towards him?

Ways of hitting and kicking the ball:

Strike the ball below the horizontal mid-line and to one side of the vertical mid-line.

Fig. 67

Try different parts of your foot to kick with but remember it is **where** you hit the ball which causes it to behave in different ways.

3. In pairs, working from one square to the other, the players start with the ball firmly wedged between their right (or left) feet. On a signal each tries to force the ball away from his partner and then to dribble it over his partner's end-line (the end-line behind him) (fig. 68).

4. Running over a fixed course, about 20 yards there and back, dribble to the end line around the skittle, turn and dribble back to stop on or over the starting line. Race in pairs until the group winner is found and then the class winner.

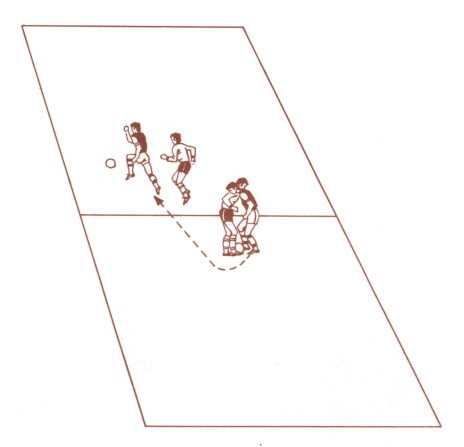

Fig. 68

Techniques for dribbling:

Start off with the ball running three or four yards in front of you but as you approach the turning mark or the stopping mark, the ball should be no more than one or two feet in front of you.

Play the ball firmly but with a loose ankle.

5. In fig. 69, working from one square to another, A and B must get past C by using interpassing movements only. They are not allowed to dribble past him. A or B may run past C to receive a forward pass. C must challenge for the ball in his opponents' square before being

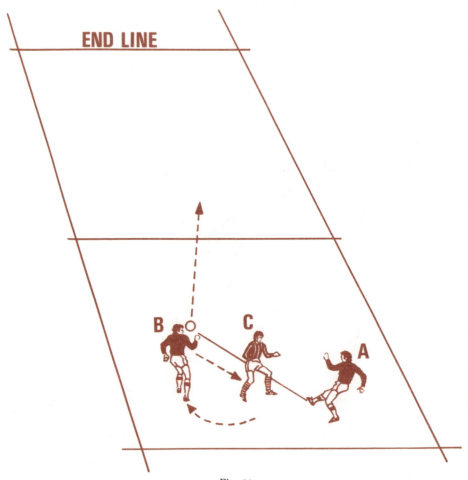

Fig. 69

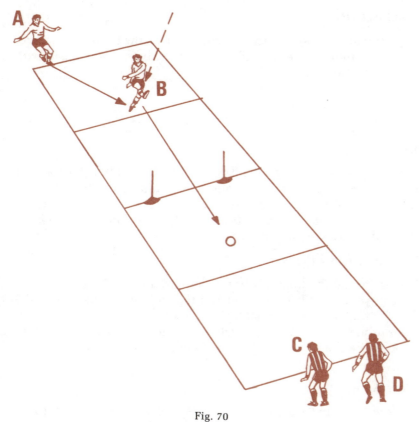

Fig. 70

allowed to make a second challenge, perhaps in his own square. A
and B try to get to C's end-line, behind him, and pick up the ball.

6. Working over 3 squares in groups of 4. In fig. 70, A serves the ball
to B. When the ball has been served into the square, B can run
forward to shoot using no more than two touches to do so. The ball is
fielded by C and D at the far end who return the practice. As
shooting improves the service from A to B can be varied—ground
passes, low bouncing balls, high thrown services and so on.

Shooting techniques:

As you control the ball push it to the side and in front of your
intended shooting foot.

Imagine a line from your shooting foot THROUGH the ball and
through the target.

Final Activity

In pairs, using a correct soccer throw-in, bring the thrown ball under control so that you need to take one pace only to stop the ball with your foot placed on top of it.

Unit 4

Introductory Activity

1 v 1 in one square. Keep the ball by dribbling it for as long as you can. Use your body to hide the ball from your partner. He must try to kick it away from you so that it leaves the square. How many times can you touch the ball with either or both feet before your opponent succeeds in kicking it out of the square?

Ways of keeping the ball:

Screen the ball by hiding it from your opponent.

Keep your body between him and the ball and dribble using the foot furthest away from him.

Position yourself so that you can see what your opponent is trying to do while keeping the ball as far from him as you can.

Class Activity

In 4's working in 2 squares. In fig. 71, A throws in to B. As A throws, C and D change position quickly. C or D calls for the ball. B must control the ball and pass to C or D (whoever has called) so that the caller doesn't have to move to stop it.

Note the following points:

While A prepares to throw in, B should try to see where C and D are out of the corner of his eye. His main attention is on A and the throw in.

After his first contact with the thrown ball B's next movement must be to turn towards the call to give the pass (unless he can back heel the ball to him safely and surely!)

Group Practices

1. 1 v 1 in one square—see Introductory Activity.

2. 8 players work in pairs in 3 squares, one ball between two. One

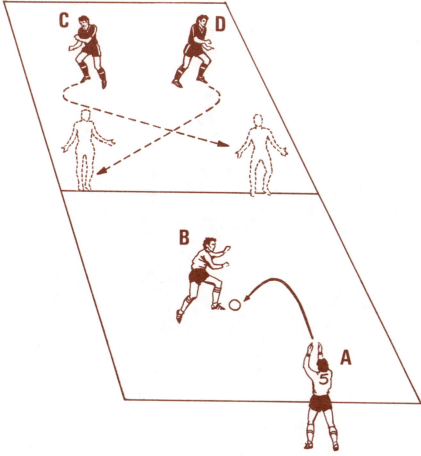

Fig. 71

player has the ball, the other runs anywhere on the pitch keeping about six or seven yards away from his partner. Any one of the free players can shout 'NOW' and when he does all the free players must stop. Following this shout the players with the balls must pass to their partners as quickly and as accurately as possible.

Remember, when you are dribbling:

Always keep your head up. Look for a target and for interference from opponents or other players who are likely to get in your way.

3. In one square—3 v 1. Three players try to keep the ball using the following sequence to do so.

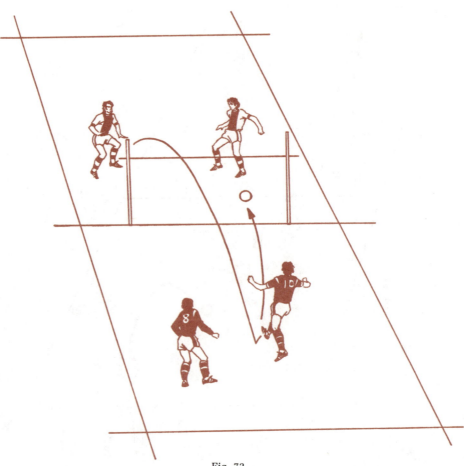

Fig. 72

A throws to B who controls the ball in the air and catches it himself. He then throws to C or A who also control the ball in the air before catching it and so on. D can intercept the pass in any way and if a player who is receiving the ball controls it badly, D may try to catch it before the other player can do so. How many passes can you score before the opposing player intercepts the ball?

4. Working in 2 squares and using high jump stands and a rope or bar to make a net 4 feet high, 4 players (2 a-side) try to build up a long return passing sequence across the net. The ball may bounce on the ground once only before it is transferred over and across the net (fig. 72).

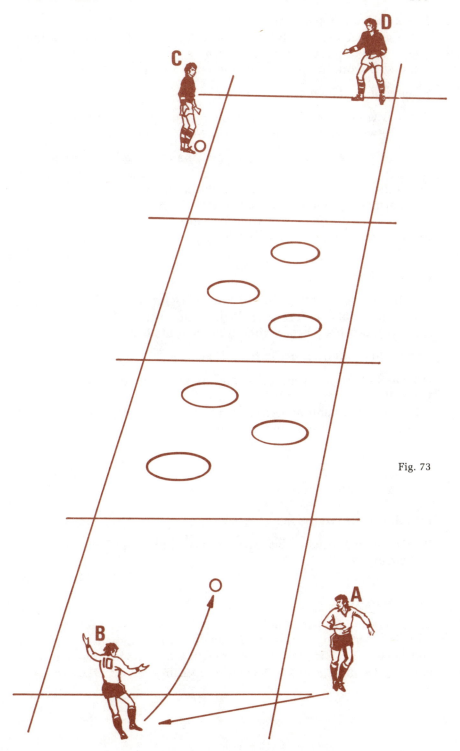

Fig. 73

5. Playing along 4 squares.

In fig. 73 A plays to B who tries to loft the ball into one of the hoops in the square furthest from him.

C and D work in the opposite direction in the same manner.

When you are kicking:

Position your body 'side on' to the target hoop. Look at the contact point between your foot and the ball NOT at the target.

6. Playing in 4 squares, 5 v 3, apply one of the following special rules.
a) Control with one foot pass with the **same** foot.
b) Control with one foot and pass with the **other** foot.
c) Pass with the outside of your foot only.
d) Pass with the point of your toe only.

Final Activity

In pairs, dodge dribbling and shadowing. Using the whole grid try to dodge and dribble to lose your shadow. On a signal all stop. Can the shadow touch his partner without moving his feet to do so?

During this activity practise the following:

Dribble so that you keep other players between your shadow and yourself.

Divide your attention between controlling the ball and looking for other players' positions and movements.

Unit 5

Introductory Activity

In 3's, in one square, heading in turn, build up long heading sequences.

Class Activity

In 3's working in 3 squares.

In fig. 74 starting in the centre square A rolls the ball to B in the end square. When the ball crosses line (2) A may move forward to try to block B's attempt to loft the ball over his head to C in the furthest

Fig. 74

square. The practice is then repeated, A passing to C from behind line (3).

As the ball rolls towards you adjust your position so that a lofted kick over A is possible as soon as the ball arrives. Having 'sighted' the target player, concentrate on striking through the vertical mid-line of the ball but well underneath the horizontal mid-line.

Group Practices—Silver Star Super Skill Tests

1. *Touch Test—juggling.*
Without using your hands or arms, keep the ball in the air for three
successive bounces then play the ball against the wall or to a partner.
Repeat the sequence of three successive bounces and again play the
ball against the wall or to your partner. After bouncing off the wall or
after being passed back to your partner the ball may be allowed to
bounce once on the ground.

   Score: 6 sequences in succession.

2. *Heading*
In pairs, A throws to B who heads back so that A can trap the ball
and finish standing with one foot on it, using only 3 touches to do
so. When B heads the ball it may bounce once only before A touches
it for the first time.

   Score: 5 out of 10.

3. *Passing*
In pairs, standing outside and playing across two empty grid squares
(20 yards), continuous passing using two touches, or less if you
wish.

   Score: 10 in succession.

4. *Controlling and trapping*
In a 10 yard grid and standing with feet wide apart, A throws to B
who controls the ball before it touches the ground. Using no more
than two further touches, B must pass the ball back to A so that the
ball passes cleanly between A's feet (fig. 75).

   Score: 8 out of 10 tries.

5. *Dribbling*
In fig. 76, starting at (A) dribble round the course shown (30 yards ×
10 yards). At (B) dribble in and out of the skittles (2 yards apart).
   At (C) play a pass off the bench (or wall).
   At (D) dribble completely round the post.
   At (E) go in and out of the skittles (2 yards apart) turn and
complete the course, as shown, to finish at (A).

   Score: 1 successful trip.

Fig. 75

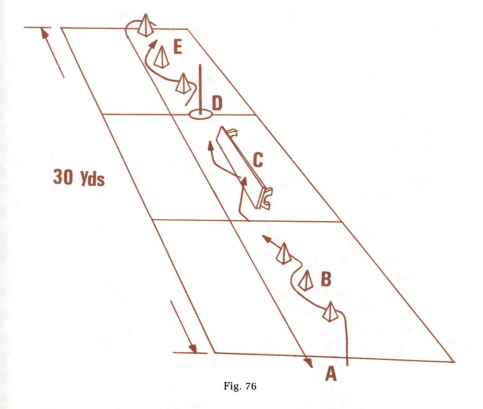

Fig. 76

6. *Kicking*

In fig. 77, A and B stand in the end squares. The ball must be kicked to clear the empty squares and the left foot and right foot must be used alternately.

Score: 6 out of 10 tries. (3 with each foot)

7. *Shooting*

Working in fours along four squares.

Standing behind B and beyond the end line of the grid, A plays a ground pass into the end square, B runs forward into the end square and shoots to score through the posts. The sequence is repeated by C and D at the other end (fig. 78).

Score: 6 out of 10 tries.

Unit 6

Introductory and Class Activity

In groups of 6, working in 3 pairs set up goals (skittles or posts) on the edges of the playing area. One pair goes into goal, the remaining two pairs play against each other to score. Whichever pair (team) scores 3 goals first, the losing pair goes into goal, the goalkeepers come out and the game of '3 goals in' continues (fig. 79).

Note the following points:

Don't worry about one game or pitch being too near to another. The players will avoid interfering with each other. Shoot as soon as you can see the goal and as soon as you are sure you can hit the target.

Place the ball wide of the goalkeeper using just enough power to beat him.

Accuracy is more important than power.

Group Practices–Silver Star Super Skill Tests

1. *Touch Test—juggling*

Without using your hands or arms, keep the ball in the air for three successive bounces then play the ball against the wall or to a partner. Repeat the sequence of three successive bounces and again play the ball against the wall or to your partner. After bouncing off the wall or

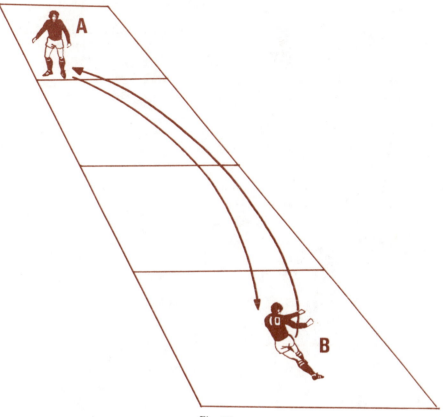

Fig. 77

after being passed back by your partner the ball may be allowed to bounce once on the ground.

Score: 6 sequences in succession.

2. Heading
In pairs, A throws to B who heads back so that A can trap the ball and finish standing with one foot on it, using only 3 touches to do so. When B heads the ball it may bounce once only before A touches it for the first time.

Score: 5 out of 10.

3. Passing
In pairs, standing outside and playing across two empty grid

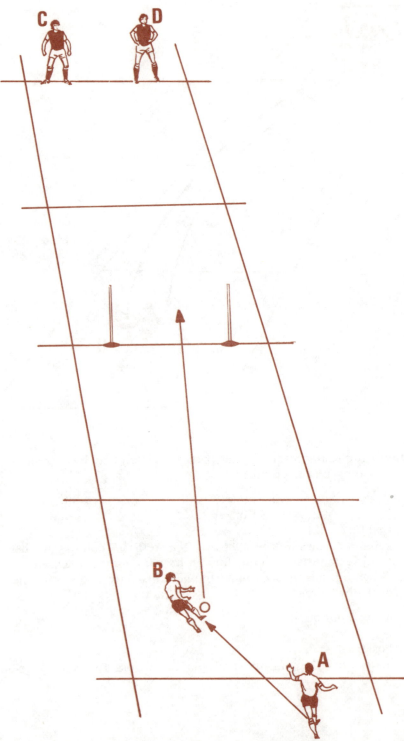

Fig. 78

Fig. 79

squares, (20 yards), practise continuous passing using two touches, or less if you wish.

Score: 10 in succession.

4. *Controlling and trapping*
In a 10 yard grid square and standing with feet wide apart, A throws to B who controls the ball before it touches the ground. Using no more than two further touches, B must pass the ball back to A so that the ball passes cleanly between A's feet.

Score: 8 out of 10 tries.

5. *Dribbling*
Starting at (A) dribble round the course shown (30 yards × 10 yards).
At (B) dribble in and out of the skittles (2 yards apart).
At (C) play a pass off the bench (or wall).

At (D) dribble completely round the post.

At (E) go in and out of the skittles (2 yards apart) turn and complete the course, as shown, to finish at (A).

Score: 1 successful trip.

6. Kicking

A and B stand in the end squares. The ball must be kicked to clear the empty squares and the left foot and right foot must be used alternately.

Score: 6 out of 10 tries. (3 with each foot)

7. Shooting

Standing behind B and beyond the end line of the grid, A plays a ground pass into the end square. B runs forward into the end square and shoots to score through the post. The sequence is repeated by C and D at the other end.

Score: 6 out of 10 tries.

VIII

12–13 Years

Unit 1

Introductory Activity

In 3's, all the players running freely in the grid, interpassing to avoid all other players with the ball and to avoid interfering with the movements of other players.

Note the following points:

Adjust your position so that you are always at the end of a clear channel down which you can pass or down which the pass can travel to you.

Always face or half face the ball so that you can receive a pass and control the ball easily and quickly.

Class Activity

1 v 1 working along two squares—tackle and dribble competition.

The ball is placed on the centre line while A and B stand on the end lines. On a signal they both run to gain possession of the ball and then try to dribble the ball over their opponent's end line. When you cross the endline flick the ball up with your foot into your hands and hold it to score a goal.

113

Techniques for tackling:

If you can't race your opponent to the ball first, try to time your approach so that as he tries to play the ball you can block it with the broad inside part of your foot and ankle.

Hold the pressure against the ball (the tackle) until you feel your opponent releasing pressure then try to force the ball away from him.

Group Practices—Silver Star Super Skill Tests

1. *Touch Test—juggling*
Without using your hands or arms keep the ball in the air for three successive bounces then play the ball against the wall or to a partner. Repeat the sequence of three successive bounces and again play the ball against the wall or to your partner. After bouncing off the wall or after being passed back by your partner, the ball may be allowed to bounce once on the ground.

   Score: 6 sequences in succession.

2. *Heading*
In pairs, A throws to B who heads back so that A can trap the ball and finish standing with one foot on it using only 3 touches to do so. When B heads the ball it may bounce once only before A touches the ball for the first time.

   Score: 5 out of 10.

3. *Passing*
In pairs, standing outside and playing across two empty grid squares, (20 yards), practise continuous passing using two touches, or less if you wish.

   Score: 10 in succession.

4. *Controlling and trapping*
In a 10 yard grid square and standing with feet wide apart, A throws to B who controls the ball before it touches the ground. Using no more than two further touches, B must pass the ball back to A so that the ball passes cleanly between A's feet.

   Score: 8 out of 10 tries.

5. *Dribbling*

Starting at (A) dribble round the course (fig. 76) shown (30 yards ×
10 yards).

At (C) play a pass off the bench (or wall).

At (D) dribble completely round the post.

At (E) go in and out of the skittles (2 yards apart) turn and
complete the course, as shown, to finish at (A).

Score: 1 successful trip.

6. *Kicking*

A and B stand in the end squares (*see* fig. 77). The ball must be
kicked to clear the empty squares and the left foot and right foot
must be used alternately.

Score: 6 out of 10 tries. (3 with each foot)

7. *Shooting* (fig. 78).

Standing behind B and beyond the end line of the grid, A plays a
ground pass into the end square. B runs forward into the end square
and shoots to score through the post. The sequence is repeated by C
and D at the other end.

Score: 6 out of 10 tries.

Unit 2

Introductory Activity

Interpassing. The whole class runs freely around the grid, in pairs,
one ball between two. Imagine ALL the other players are opponents
and try to interpass with your partner so that you go past them using
a sequence of first time passes to do so. These are known as wall
passes or 'one-two's'.

Everyone practise wall passes or 'one-two's' against everyone else.

Class Activity

Volleying for distance and accuracy

Working along and outside two squares, A throws the ball into the
air and in front of him. As the ball bounces A waits until the ball is at
a suitable height for him to kick the ball to his partner WHILE IT IS

IN THE AIR. Try to drop the ball into your partner's arms as if he were a goalkeeper.

Techniques for volleying:

Point your toe and keep your ankle firm. Swing your foot from the knee and hit the ball with the laces on your shoe.

Can you change your body position so that you can volley the ball even when it is quite high in the air? That's right, turn sideways on to the ball and lean or fall away from it (fig. 80).

Fig. 80

Group Practices

1. 1 v 1 tackle and dribble contests.
2. 1 v 1, standing behind a mark on the ground A heads as far as he can over or towards B. B heads back from the point at which A's header first strikes the ground. A follows the same procedure. How far back can you drive your partner by heading beyond him? Each successive header takes place from where the previous header to you first touches the ground.

Techniques for heading:

Head the ball upwards and away.

Use your legs to throw your trunk and head at and through the ball.

3. 1 v 1 in one square. A tries to turn past B to cross the line behind him (fig. 81).

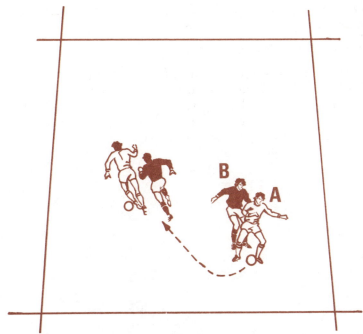

Fig. 81

4. In 3's, 2 v 1. A and B try to dribble or interpass past C to get into C's square and to cross the END-LINE before he can get in a second or third tackle or challenge. When they take the ball over the end-line A or B must flick up the ball, using his feet, so that one or the other catches the ball in the air to score (fig. 82).

5. *Long throw-in competition.*
Using a correct soccer throw in, organise group and class competitions for distance.

6. *Shooting*
In fig. 83, keeping outside the four squares, both teams try to knock down the largest number of skittles. 4 balls in play only.

Final Activity

Free dribbling in the grid. While dribbling try to kick everyone else's ball out of the grid. When your ball is out you are out. Who is the last one left in?

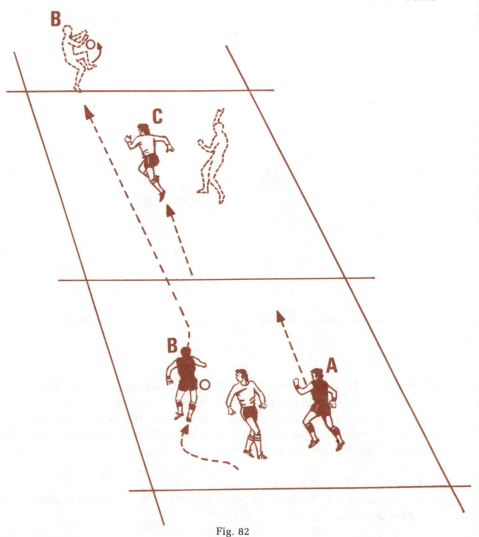

Fig. 82

Unit 3

Introductory Activity

One player to one ball or two players to one ball. Practise juggling sequences:

e.g. left foot, right foot scores one.
or   left foot, right thigh scores one.
or   head, thigh, foot scores one.

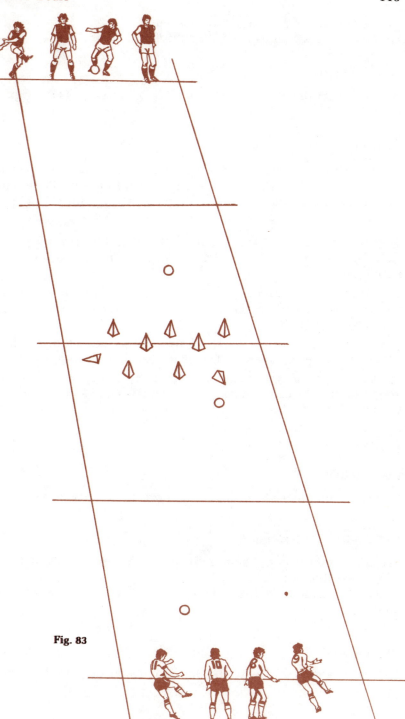

Fig. 83

How many can you do in unbroken sequence?
Group and class records can be established.

Class Activity

6 v 6 competitions on a pitch 40 yards × 30 yards (4 × 3 grid
squares).

Group Practices

1. Speed dribbling along 4 square course. In and out of the pair of
skittles, around the single skittle and return from the single end
skittle in a straight run with the ball to the starting line (fig. 84).

2. 2 v 2 v 2. Three goals in.

3. Target shooting in 4 squares. In fig. 85, A and B serve to C who
shoots to score past D. E, F and G are retrievers. Change the positions
from time to time.

4. In groups of 4, keep the ball in the air for the greatest number of
bounces. No player may play the ball twice in succession. The ball
must not touch the ground.

5. In groups of 4, 2 a-side, build up long sequences of headed
passes. No player, on one side, may play the ball twice in succession.

6. In pairs, one player stands with his feet wide apart, while the
other tries to play a ground pass under the bridge. The players move
further apart to find the longest accurate push pass.

Unit 4

Class Activity

3 v 3 Competition played on a pitch 30 yards × 20 yards (3 squares ×
2).

Practise triangle techniques:

Try to play for triangle positions. They give the best passing and the
best supporting positions.

Change positions in the triangle to try to upset the defending
opponents.

Group Activities

1. In 4 squares, 4 × 4 with the opposing teams paired off against

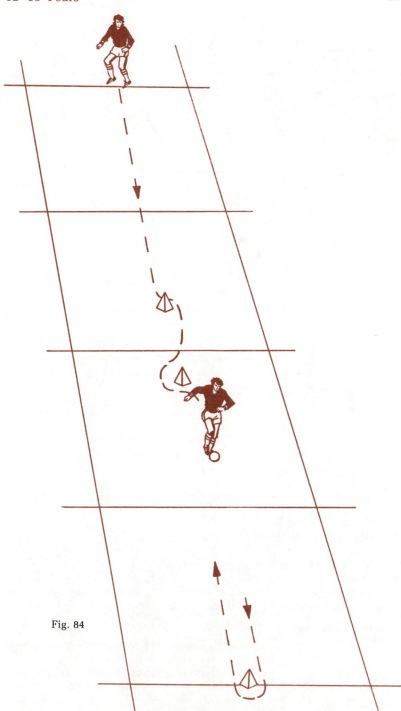

Fig. 84

Fig. 85

each other (fig. 86). One player only from each team may position himself in each square. Keep the ball—how many unbroken passes can each team achieve?

Practise the following tactics:

If the ball looks like coming to you, try to imagine where and when your team mate intends to pass the ball then dodge away from the line of the pass before returning to it quickly. Draw your opponent away from the space into which the ball can be passed.

2. In 4's alternate long and short passes.

In fig. 87, A plays a long pass to B on line 4. B plays a short return pass to D who plays long to C.

C plays a long pass to D on line 3 who passes short to B who plays long to C and so on.

3. In 2 squares and using high jump stands and a rope to make a net, play 2 v 2, Soccer Tennis. The ball is allowed to bounce once only on the ground before it must be played back over the net. Score as for table tennis. Serve by heading, throwing or kicking over the net from behind the end line.

4. Dribbling 'up the ladder' competition. In fig. 88 starting behind

Fig. 86

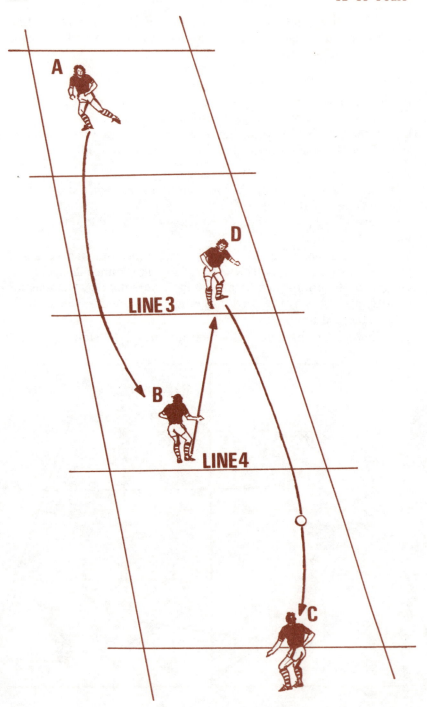

Fig. 87

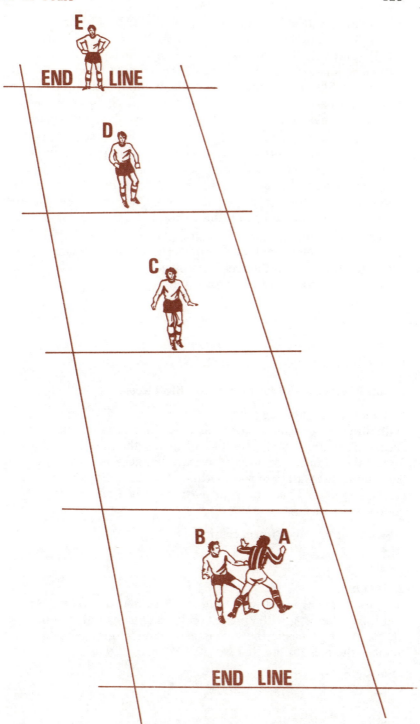

END LINE

END LINE

Fig. 88

the end line, A dribbles into the first square. As soon as he enters the square B may move forward to challenge. If A beats B he can move into the second square and again, as soon as he enters the square, C may move forward into the square to challenge. A tries to 'climb the ladder' until he reaches the far end line without losing the ball and without the ball leaving the channel of squares. In the early stages, a tackler may make only one challenge for the ball in his square.

5. Working over 6 squares, in fig. 89, C and D interpass so that they can pass over the empty squares to G and H who try to do the same. Each time the ball crosses the empty squares, from one half of a team to the other half, the team scores one. Should the other team gain possession they try to achieve the same kind of sequence. The ball can be played in the air or on the ground.

6. Working **along** 6 squares, in pairs, players try to volley the ball, keeping it in the channel all the time. The player volleying the ball tries to do this, so that the receiving player can catch the ball taking no more than one step in any direction to do so.

Units 5 and 6

Group Practices—Silver Star Super Skill Tests

1. *Touch Test—juggling*
Without using your hands or arms keep the ball in the air for three successive bounces then play the ball against the wall or to a partner. Repeat the sequence of three successive bounces and again play the ball against the wall or to your partner. After bouncing off the wall or after being passed back by your partner the ball may be allowed to bounce once on the ground.

Score: 6 sequences in succession.

2. *Heading*
In pairs, A throws to B who heads back so that A can trap the ball and finish standing with one foot on the ball using only 3 touches to do so. When B heads the ball it may bounce once only before A touches the ball for the first time.

Score: 5 out of 10.

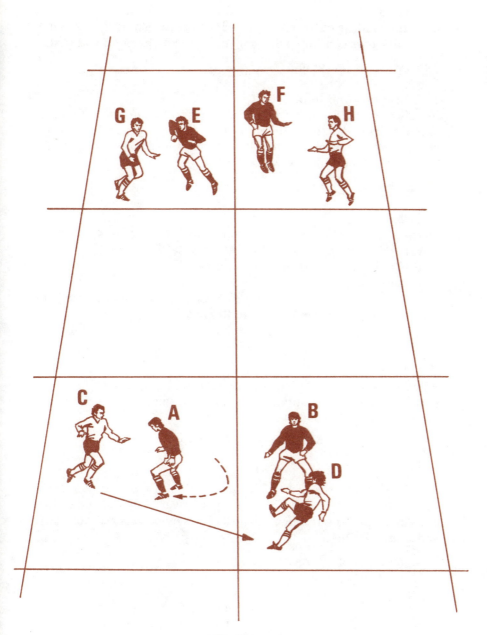

Fig. 89

3. *Passing*

In pairs, standing outside and playing across two empty grid squares (20 yards), pass continuously using two touches, or less if you wish.

Score: 10 in succession.

4. *Controlling and trapping*

In a 10 yard grid square and standing with feet wide apart, A throws to B who controls the ball before it touches the ground. Using no more than two further touches, B must pass the ball back to A so that the ball passes cleanly between A's feet.

Score: 8 out of 10 tries.

5. *Dribbling*

Starting at (A) dribble round the course shown (30 yards × 10 yards).

At (B) dribble in and out of the skittles (2 yards apart).

At (C) play a pass off the bench (or wall).

At (D) dribble completely round the post.

At (E) go in and out of the skittles (2 yards apart) turn and complete the course, as shown, to finish at (A).

Score: 1 successful trip.

6. *Kicking*

A and B stand in the end squares (see the diagram). The ball must be kicked to clear the empty squares and the left foot and right foot must be used alternately.

Score: 6 out of 10 tries. (3 with each foot)

7. *Shooting*

Standing behind B and beyond the end line of the grid, A plays a ground pass into the end square. B runs forward into the end square and shoots to score through the post. The sequence is repeated by C and D at the other end.

Score: 6 out of 10 tries.

IX

13–14 Years

Unit 1

Introductory Activity (10 minutes)

In pairs, working across the grid and outside the two square central channel, A kicks to B so that the ball clears both squares. B controls the ball in

    (a) three touches

or (b) two touches

or (c) one touch

and then drives the ball on the ground across the channel to A. Repeat and change over.

Note the following kicking techniques:

When kicking with your right foot, point your left shoulder towards your partner as you swing your kick through and under the ball towards him. For tight control, relax the controlling surface and let it give with the ball as contact is made. To drive the ball along the ground keep the knee of your kicking leg over the ball, toe down and your ankle firm.

Class Activity (10–18 minutes)

In 4's, working over three squares, A kicks to B, B controls the ball and combines with C to try to score against A and D (fig. 90). A and D

Fig. 90

may only enter B and C's square when the receiving player has touched the ball once. Use small goals or goals made of skittles, posts or cricket stumps. These may be 5 feet wide or smaller. Change positions after three or four attempts.

Game Practices

If you have only one pitch, half the class plays 7 v 7 (±) and the other half plays 3 v 3 (±) as shown on the pitch diagram. After 20–25 minutes the half classes changes over. Classes should be organized so that in game practices or team competitions the teams have the good and not so good players shared equally.

The games will be used to emphasize principles of play, e.g. support in attacking play. Support in attack is best produced from a triangular relationship between three or more players (fig. 91a). The distances between the players should make accurate passing between them easy. As a player receives the ball the positions of his team mates should present him with the greatest range of passing possibilities. The positions of players within the triangle can

Fig. 91a

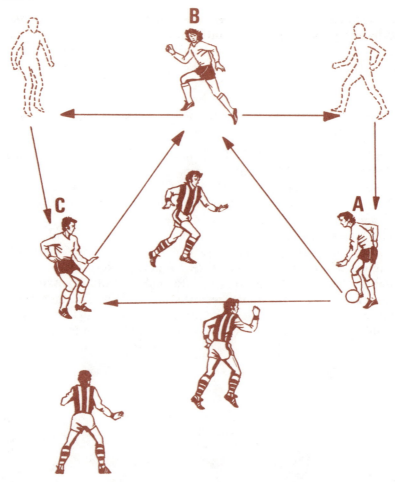

Fig. 91b

change. The shape of the triangle can change but the flatter the triangle, generally speaking, the greater the risk of passes being intercepted. Teachers should emphasize the principle of support in all team situations. An increase in the number of players merely provides more opportunities for inter-related triangles (fig. 91b).

Unit 2

Introductory Activity

In pairs, working across and outside the two square central channel,

A throws to B using a correct soccer throw in. B heads back to A who controls and gives a return ground pass using:

   (a) three touches
or (b) two touches
or (c) a first time pass.

   If the throwing distance is too great, work across and outside a one square channel.

Class Activity

In 4's (fig. 92), A kicks over the two squares to B who heads to C. B

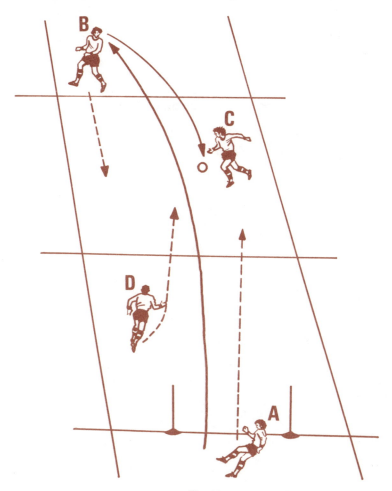

Fig. 92

and C interpass to score against A and D. A and D may enter B and C's square only when B has headed the ball. Change the positions and functions after three or four attempts.

Use the following techniques:

B, the player receiving the kicked pass, tries to anticipate the line of the kick from A's approach to the ball. When heading, nod through the ball towards the target player OR as the ball contacts your forehead, point your forehead towards the target player and allow your head to give with the ball as contact is made. This second technique enables a player to take pace off the ball and to drop it at the feet of a nearby team-mate.

Game Practice

7 v 7 (±) and 3 v 3 (±) as previously.

This unit of work illustrates and emphasizes the need for attacking on a wide front to create space among opponents.

In fig. 93, A, B and C have achieved good supporting positions. A

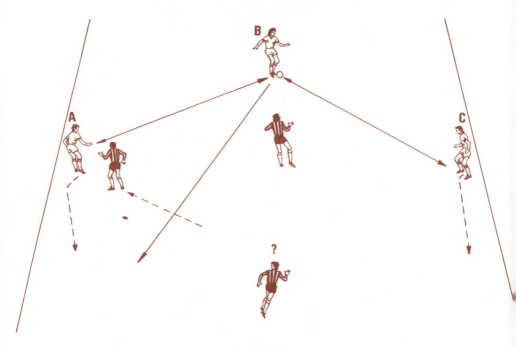

Fig. 93

and C have moved wide of B. Opponents know that central space is the area from which effective shots can be made and that if they move wide they cannot cover central space. If the opponents don't move wide then A or C may receive the ball and make progress down the wings. A major factor in judging understanding in any team passing game is the degree to which players appreciate how their movements into and out of certain parts of the field can set very difficult problems for opponents. When should they mark opponents and when should they cover dangerous spaces?

It doesn't matter who moves into wide positions when your team has the ball so long as someone moves there. Players should be encouraged to exchange and interchange positions freely and sensibly.

Unit 3

Introductory Activity

In pairs, working in two squares and using cones or skittles as goals—4 feet, 3 feet or 2 feet apart. Taking it in turns A or B dribble into each other's square from which they may attempt a shot at goal. A shot may be taken only when the dribbling player has made at least one attempt to trick or to dribble past his opponent.

Class Activity

In 4's, (fig. 94), two facing two, outside the one square central channel, A throws in the air to B and runs to the end of B's team. B controls the ball and passes to C. B runs to the end of C's team.

C catches the ball and throws to D. C runs to the end of D's team and so on.

Pay close attention to the need for accuracy in ball contact whatever the technique being used. All passes and throws should be delivered firmly but softly so that a receiving player has few problems in controlling or stopping the ball.

Game Practice

7 v 7 and 3 v 3 as previously.

Techniques for attacking play:

Attacking play must involve moving the ball accurately and quickly

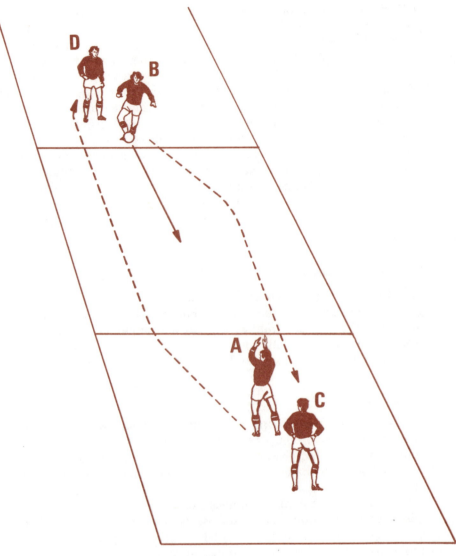

Fig. 94

into positions from which accurate shots can be taken. Attacking teams must penetrate (get behind) opposing defences sooner rather than later by interpassing or dribbling.

Unit 4

Introductory Activity

In two squares, 3 against 1. The three players in possession may use only one (two) touches to establish the highest unbroken sequence of passes. If the single player touches the ball, or if the ball leaves the square, he takes the place of the player in the three who caused it to happen.

Note the following points:

If you are near to the player who has the ball make a good passing angle for him.

If you are not near to the player who has the ball anticipate where he will pass and show a good passing angle for the player who you think may receive it (fig. 95).

Class Activity

In 4's, (fig. 96), two against two, working across the two square central channel, A drives or lofts a kick to B. B must give a first time pass to C. When he has touched the ball A and D may challenge for the ball by entering B and C's square if they wish. B and C try to score through the goal at the other end of the pitch.

Note the following techniques:

Look for the position of your team mate before the ball comes to you.

Having sighted your target player, the player to whom you intend to pass the ball, concentrate on an accurate contact through the ball towards your partner.

If an opponent is nearby, take pace off the ball as you pass by relaxing and even withdrawing the passing surface slightly.

Game Practice

7 v 7 and 3 v 3. Against players who know how to defend by covering each other and marking opponents, it is important to understand where and when to change positions so that they (the defenders) have problems in marking and covering effectively.

In fig. 97, showing one half of a pitch marked out in imaginary zones, the numbers indicate the importance of those zones to a defending team. The lower the number the more important the zone; the higher the number the less important the zone. The arc projected

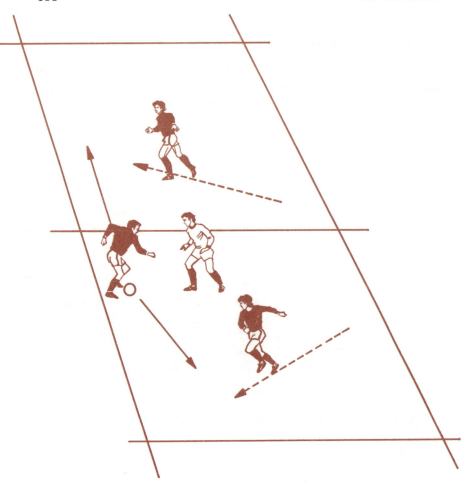

Fig. 95

from the goal indicates that part of the pitch from which attackers are most likely to score. The area may be smaller according to the age, skill and power of the players but, broadly speaking, the statement is true for all pitches and for all players. It follows that attackers who spend most of their time (and energy) in high number areas will be less effective (less dangerous) than those who try to get possession in low number areas. Attacking play to score goals begins to make sense when players are taught to move out of the low number areas ONLY when a team mate wants to move into them and

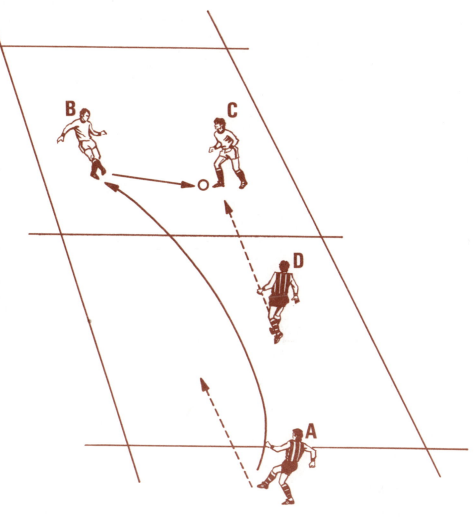

Fig. 96

when, by moving out, they can draw defenders with them. Occasionally, of course, a central attacking player will ignore the above rule when he moves out of central dangerous areas to help (support) a team mate who is in trouble.

Interchanging positions is known as MOBILITY. Attacking play against good defence must involve attackers interchanging positions with each other. Running all over the place all the time without thought or purpose is, of course, bad play.

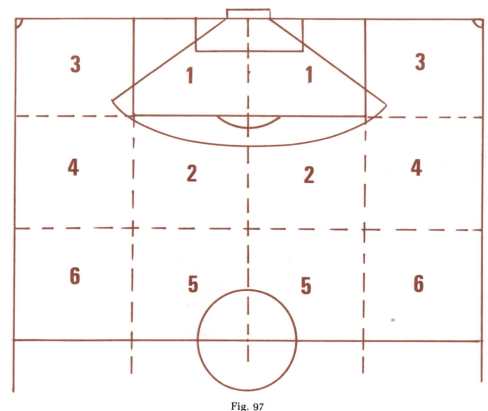

Fig. 97

Unit 5

Introductory Activity

In 4's working across and outside the two square channels. In fig. 98, B plays a ground pass to A who gives a controlled return ground pass. B hits a long lofted pass over the two squares to C. C controls the ball and plays a short pass to D who gives a return ground pass. C hits a long lofted pass to B who controls and so on. Change positions.

Group Practices—Gold Star Super Skill Tests

1. *Touch Test—juggling*
In a 10 yard grid square, by yourself, keep the ball in the air

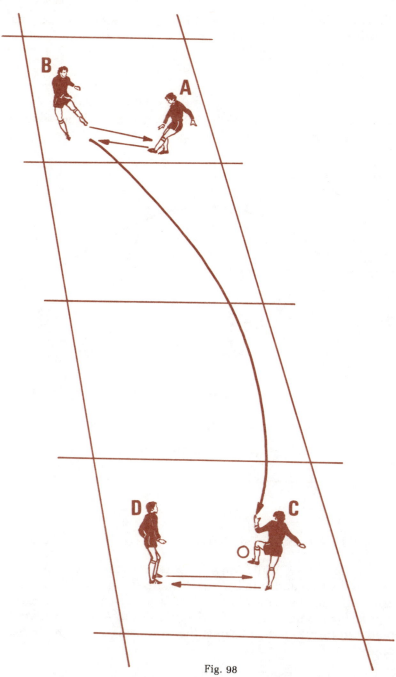

Fig. 98

continuously but this time you cannot use the same part of your body twice in succession. Your hands and arms **cannot be used.**

Score: 8 bounces in succession.

2. *Heading*
In fig. 99, standing outside a 10 yard grid square and playing across it, A throws to B who heads back so that A can control the ball and pass it back to B within 2 touches, one to control and one to pass back.

Score: 5 in succession.

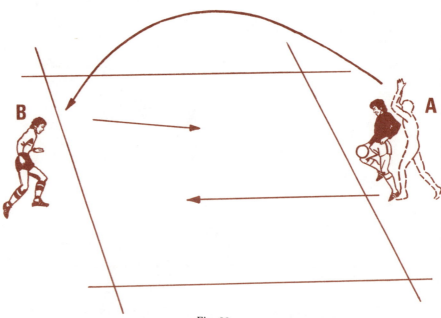

Fig. 99

3. *Passing*
In pairs A, facing the wall, throws to B who is standing 5 yards or more from the wall and with his back towards it (fig. 100). B controls the ball, turns and passes against the wall below the 2 foot wall mark. B controls the rebound and passes the ball back to A. B must control the ball and turn to pass it against the wall using not more than 3 touches.

Score: 10 in succession.

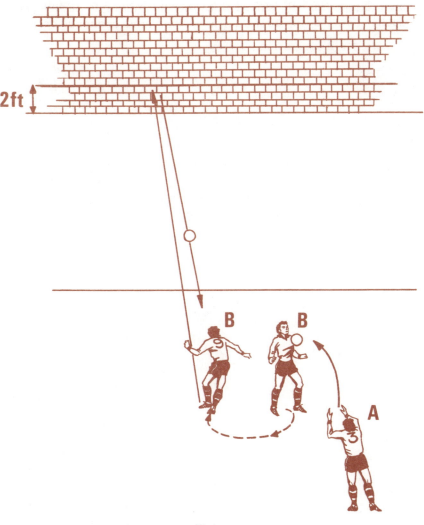

2ft

Fig. 100

Alternative Passing Test 3. In 4's, A and B face C and D standing no less than 5 yards away. C has his back to A and B but faces D some yards away.

D throws to C using a controlled football throw in. C controls the ball and within two more touches (three in all) C must turn and pass to A or B 5 yards away. A and B return pass to C who controls and turns to pass the ball back to D once again using a maximum of 3 touches to do so (fig. 101).

Score: 10 in succession.

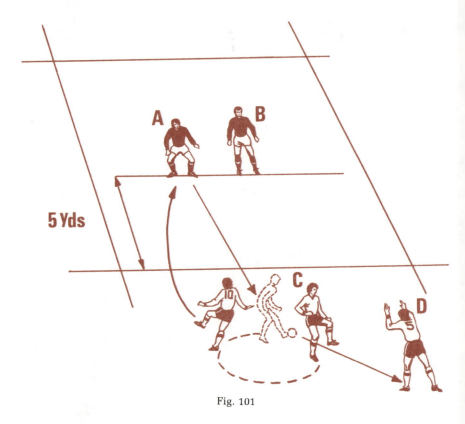

Fig. 101

4. *Controlling and trapping*
In a 10 yard grid square A, standing with feet wide apart, throws to B who controls the ball before it touches the ground. After controlling the ball with one touch, one more touch only may be used by B to play the ball back to A and through his legs. A maximum of 2 touches must be used to control and pass the ball.

Score: 8 out of 10 tries.

5. *Dribbling*
In fig. 102, starting at (A), dribble round the course shown. At (B) dribble in and out of the skittles 2 yards apart. At (C) play a pass off

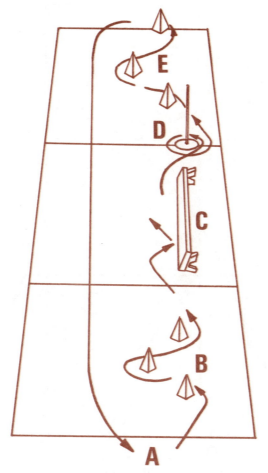

Fig. 102

the bench or the wall as shown. At (D) dribble completely round the post. At (E) go in and out of the skittles and finish at (A)

Score: 2 trips.

6. *Kicking*

A, B, C, D are positioned as in fig. 103. C rolls a short pass to A who kicks the ball first time to the diagonal player B. The ball must pass over the empty square between, without touching the ground. B repeats the sequence so that D kicks the ball first time diagonally to

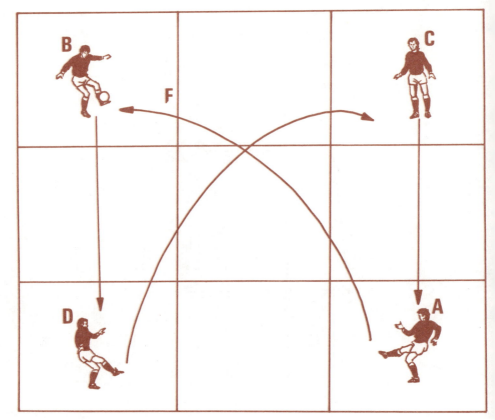

Fig. 103

C. The players change over to enable C and B to be tested. When the ball is kicked to a player he must control the ball within his square without using hand or arm to do so.

Score: 7 out of 10 tries.

7. *Shooting*
In fig. 104, A stands behind B and beyond the end line of the grid, throwing the ball to bounce in the end square. B must control the ball in that square and shoot to score in 2 touches or less. The sequence can be repeated by C and D at the other end.

Score: 7 out of 10 tries.

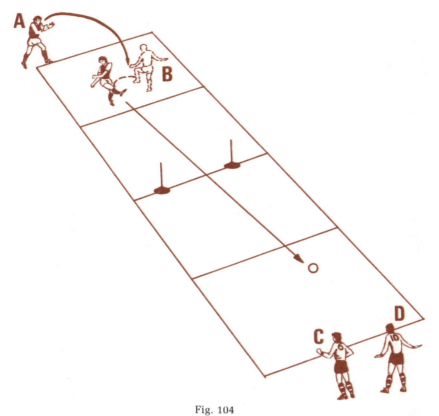

Fig. 104

Unit 6

Introductory Activity

In 4's work across and outside the two square channel as in fig. 98. A plays a short ground pass to B who collects the pass with one touch and with only a second touch hits a long pass to C who controls the ball.

C passes to D who, using two touches, hits a long pass to B who controls and passes to A and so on. The sequence is repeated and the players change over when appropriate.

Group Practices—Gold Star Super Skill Tests

1. *Touch Test—juggling*
In a 10 yard grid square, by yourself, keep the ball in the air

continuously, but this time you cannot use the same part of your body twice in succession. Your hands and arms **cannot** be used.

Score: 8 bounces in succession.

2. Heading

Standing outside a 10 yard grid square and playing across it, A throws to B who heads back so that A can control the ball and pass it back to B within 2 touches, one to control and one to pass back.

Score: 5 in succession.

3. Passing

In pairs A, facing the wall, throws to B who is standing 5 yards or more from the wall and with his back towards it. B controls the ball, turns and passes against the wall below the 2 foot wall mark. B controls the rebound and passes the ball back to A. B must control the ball and turn to pass it against the wall using not more than 3 touches.

Score: 10 in succession.

Alternative Passing Test 3. In fours, A and B face C and D standing no less than 5 yards away. C has his back to A and B but faces D some yards away.

D throws to C using a controlled football throw in. C controls the ball and within two more touches (three in all) C must turn and pass to A or B five yards away. A and B return pass to C who controls and turns to pass the ball back to D once again using a maximum of 3 touches to do so.

Score: 10 in succession.

4. Controlling and trapping

In a 10 yard grid square A, standing with feet wide apart, throws to B who controls the ball before it touches the ground. After controlling the ball with one touch, one more touch only may be used by B to play the ball back to A and through his legs. A maximum of 2 touches must be used to control and pass the ball.

Score: 8 out of 10 tries.

5. Dribbling

Starting at (A) dribble round the course shown. At (B) dribble in and out of the skittles 2 yards apart. At (C) play a pass off the bench or the wall as shown. At (D) dribble completely round the post. At (E) go in and out of the skittles and finish at (A) (fig. 102).

Score: 2 trips.

6. *Kicking*

A, B, C, D are positioned as in the diagram (fig. 103). C rolls a short pass to A who kicks the ball first time to the diagonal player B. The ball must pass over the empty square between, without touching the ground. B repeats the sequence so that D kicks the ball first time diagonally to C. The players change over to enable C and B to be tested. When the ball is kicked to a player he must control the ball within his square without using hand or arm to do so.

Score: 7 out of 10 tries.

7. *Shooting*

Standing behind B and beyond the end line of the grid (fig. 104). A throws the ball to bounce in the end square. B must control the ball in that square and shoot to score in 2 touches or less.

The sequence can be repeated by C and D at the other end.

Score: 7 out of 10 tries.

X

14–15 Years

Unit 1

Introductory Activity

In 4's, two facing two, across and outside the two square channels (fig. 105).

A hits a lofted pass to B and follows his pass to a position behind D.

B controls the ball and hits a lofted pass to C and follows his pass to a position behind C.

C controls the ball and hits a lofted pass to D and so on—pass and run to change ends continuously.

Class Activities

In fig. 106, practice begins with the free attackers (e.g. White 7–11) taking up standing positions anywhere in their attacking half of the pitch. Defending players (black) take up positions accordingly to mark and cover. Feeders, white 4–6, can play the ball to each other in the channel and, when it suits them, play the ball to one or other of their attackers. White 4–6, the feeders, cannot take part in attacking play by moving out of the central channel. Forward players, if under pressure from opponents, may play the ball back to the feeders.

Attack versus defence situations of this kind can be used to

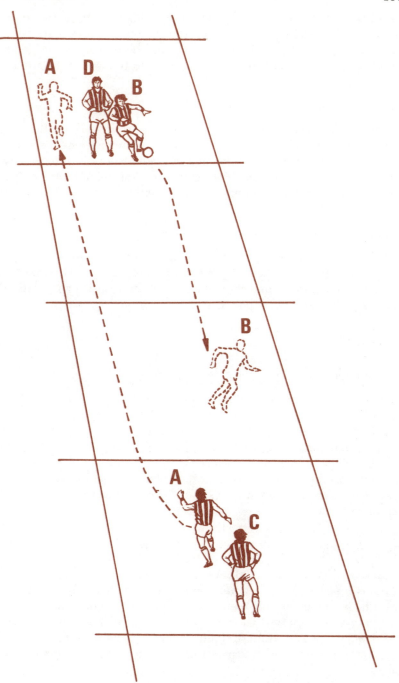

Fig. 105

develop an understanding of the need for players to help each other in both defence and attack. In the illustration 26 players are being coached on one pitch. The numbers could be bigger. When defenders win the ball they must try to return it to the feeders accurately and quickly.

Use the following techniques:

If the attacker nearest to you is not likely to receive the ball, cover your nearest team-mate and keep an eye on your opponent's movement. Cover and support in defence is a matter of tight interlocking triangles. When one defender is beaten another defender (covering) can instantly contain the danger of a breakthrough.

Game Practice

11 v 11—looking for opportunities to apply and relate the principle of support (depth) in the full game. Stop play from time to time, but not too often, so that players can examine their positional relationships and the triangular patterns between them.

Unit 2

Introductory Activity

In 4's or 6's working across the two square channel, two facing two. A drives, chips or lofts the ball towards B as if shooting. A follows his shot to join the end of B's team. B saves by catching or fielding the ball and throws (goalkeeper style) to C. B follows his throw to join C's team.

C controls the ball and drives, chips or lofts the ball to D and so on. After each kick or throw the kicker or thrower runs to the end of the opposite team.

Class Activity

Attack v Defence fig. 106. As previously except that both the supporting players, e.g. White 4 and 6, can move freely to support the attack. The defending team tries to produce superior numbers of players (twos or threes) wherever the ball is. Defenders try to make the attackers pass in front of them. The defenders' aim is to prevent attackers moving into positions from which effective shots can be taken.

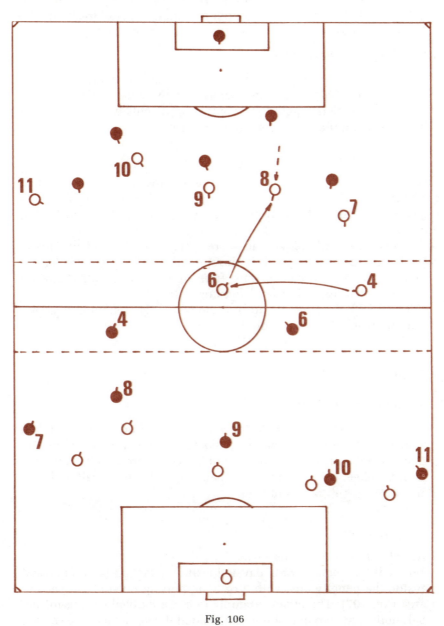

Fig. 106

When the defending team wins the ball they can score by building up an interpassing sequence of six uninterrupted passes which must end with a lofted kick into the mid-field zone. The attacking side must work hard to hustle opponents and try to break up the interpassing sequence to regain possession of the ball.

Try the following techniques:

When faced by a player in possession of the ball try to guide him towards one of his team-mates whom you know to be well marked.

If in doubt or if caught between two opponents with the ball, fall back until another defender can support you.

Game Practice

11 v 11—develop the principles of depth and concentration when defending. When attacking try to stretch defenders as much as possible by taking them away from each other. Apply the following RULE.

A team can only shoot and score when the whole of that team, excluding the goalkeeper, is in the opposing half of the field. A team can only move the ball forward from its defending half when the whole of that team is in its defending half of the field.

This RULE develops the idea of the whole team moving to attack and the whole team defending as a unit.

Unit 3

Introductory Activity

7 v 4 in one half of the field the seven try to build up an unbroken sequence of 10, 15 or 20 passes. Adjust the number of defenders (6 v 5, 8 v 3 and so on) to suit the skill of the larger group in keeping the ball. Goalkeepers must use their hands to collect the ball and may throw or kick it to a team mate.

Class Activity

Attack v Defence—corner kicks
With a full defence (7 or 8 players) position attackers (4 or 5 players) inside the penalty area with 2 or 3 supporting outside the penalty area (fig. 107). The attack attempts to score by challenging for the ball delivered into one of the four shaded danger areas. The shaded

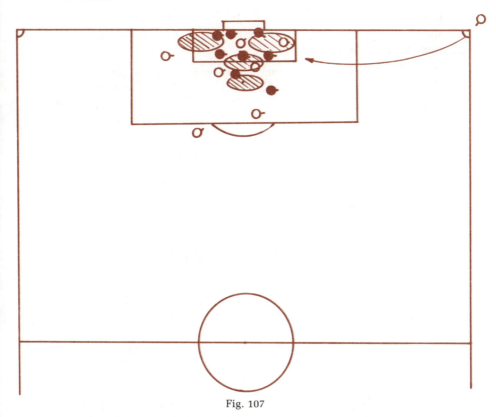

Fig. 107

areas close to the goal-lines should be attacked using inswinging corners, the others using outswinging corners.

Game Practice

11 v 11—during periods when one team or the other is defending, award a corner kick to the attacking team, even though the ball hasn't gone out of play, to test the understanding of the organization established in the Class Activity.

For short periods say 2 or 3 minutes apply the following:
when you make a pass to a team mate you MUST follow your own pass. Failure to do so means that the ball will be given to your opponent.

This is a good teaching point to emphasize the need to think ALWAYS in terms of helping your team mates by moving towards them.

Unit 4

Introductory Activities

In pairs, two pairs to one square, tackle and dribble competition.
1. The players begin with their non-tackling foot against the ball and their tackling foot one pace back. On an agreed signal both players strike for the ball and try to dribble it over their opponent's end line.
2. As previously but both players begin with feet together one full stride away from the ball.
3. As previously but both players begin outside the end lines of the square.
4. As in 3. with backs to each other. The ball is bounced or rolled into position equidistant between them. The players turn and challenge for the ball.

Note the following points:

Time the strike of your foot to coincide with your opponent's. Hold pressure against the ball until you feel your opponent relaxing his pressure.

Having lost the first tackle, perhaps, be quick in recovery to get in your second tackle.

Class Activity

Attack v Defence. A goalkeeper and 5, 6 or 7 defenders against attackers with one extra player. The attackers (with the extra player) try to produce two attackers against one defender wherever the ball happens to be. When the two against one situation has been achieved the attackers try to pass the defender by quick interpassing or by dribbling.

Attack v Defence techniques:

Any player not marked by an opponent must move quickly to the player with the ball.

Use the extra player to make progress not merely to keep possession without progress.

Game Practice

11 v 11—both teams should try to play accurate short passing football so that the players have opportunities to make the spare

player situations. The following rule will assist in creating these situations:

No pass allowed above knee height.

Reference can also be made to the need to pass and follow your own pass, to create play in which the player on the ball has adequate support.

Unit 5

Introductory Activity

In 4's, or any number greater than 4, throw, control, pass (fig. 108).

A throws to B who controls with his chest, thigh, instep, head etc.

As each player throws the ball or controls and passes it he runs to the end of the opposite team.

Fig. 108

Class Activity

2 v 2 v 2—'Three goals in' The goal is made of skittles or posts and is 12 yards wide. Two players keep goal and the remaining four players play 2 v 2 to score. The team which scores three goals makes its opponents go into goal. Goals are only allowed below the height of the skittles or the posts.

Use the following techniques in this activity:

When your side has the ball, move away from the ball threatening to move round the back of your opponent, then move quickly towards the ball to make a two against one situation or to gain shooting space.

Shoot as soon as you can see the target and hit it. When near to goal ALWAYS EXPECT the ball to come and position yourself so that WHEN it comes you can hit the ball and the target INSTANTLY.

Game Practices

7 v 7 and 3 v 3—these games will be used to emphasize or re-emphasize the principles of play and the fundamental elements of the game. They will be more effectively used if RULES are imposed:

1. One sideways or backwards pass MUST be followed by a forward pass.
2. Pass and run past the nearest opponent towards his goal.
3. When you receive the ball you MUST attack the nearest opponent between you and their goal.
4. When you receive the ball immediately place your body between the ball and your nearest opponent.

Unit 6

Introductory Activity

Speed dribbling relays. In teams of 4, 6 or 8, split into two halves facing each other, working from the penalty area to the centre circle. The players dribbling the ball must stop the ball by putting the sole of the foot on the ball in the receiving player's box. The outgoing player may not touch the ball until this has been done. Set each player a number of trips; e.g. each player must make 6 trips.

Class Activities

Attack v Defence. These practice situations will involve the attacking exploitation of throws in, free kicks and corner kicks. The attacking players will outnumber the defending outfield players by one or two.

Suggested numbers are seven attackers against six defenders. Defenders and attackers change over after each two or three practice runs.

The objects of a throw in are:

1. To keep possession of the ball and make progress towards goal.
2. To use a player's special skill, e.g. a very long throw, to create danger near to goal.

Free kicks near to goal should result in an accurate shot on goal within one or two touches. Free kicks further from goal should result in the ball being moved forward with a view to a shot on goal taking place as soon as possible.

Game Practice

Team Competition. 11 v 11, or numbers as appropriate to the total numbers in the class. The games will be stopped every 10 minutes for coaching purposes. Coaching points made will be general and for the benefit of players in both teams.

XI

15–16 Years

Unit 1

In this age group the players will be streamed according to their
levels of skill, for some of the year's work at least. We may assume
that half the class is capable of playing eleven a side football in a
competent manner and with a reasonable degree of understanding.
Less able players will spend half their time in either small sided
games or game situations using the coaching grid and the remaining
half in 11 a-side football.

Introductory Activity

In threes (or fours) 2 v 1 or 3 v 1 in two squares, keep the ball
practice. 10 unbroken passes = 1 goal.

Always imagine that the ball will come to you next—even if it
seems unlikely—and position yourself accordingly. Having anticipated the ball coming in your direction, think of two things which
you can do when it comes. Ask yourself the following questions:

Who can I pass to?
Have I got enought time (space) to control the ball?
Shall I pretend to pass and dribble?
Where can I move to, to be ready for the next pass or the one after
that?

Class Activity and Game Practice

5 v 5 or 4 v 4 on the area normally used for 7 v 7 (e.g. 70 yards × 30 yards approximately). Where possible, pitches should be specially marked out and small goals with nets should be provided. Players who are not so skilful need extra motivation and encouragement.

Almost certainly ineffectiveness in football springs from a lack of confidence in bringing the ball under control quickly and surely. Usually this is caused by trying to share attention between the ball, team mates and opponents. Only very skilful players can do this.

The following techniques will help improve control:

As the ball comes towards you imagine a line through the ball to that part of your body you intend to use to bring the ball under control.

Let the ball hit you and watch it all the way onto the part of your body you are using to control it.

As soon as you have made the first contact with the ball try to play it again away from your standing position and follow it quickly.

Competitions

The trouble taken to organize league competitions for small sided teams for the players will pay you well. Publish results, goal scorers and the league tables, even better give boys the responsibility for organizing these affairs.

Technique Practice

A perceptive teacher will see when there is a need for basic practice and will stop game form activities occasionally to set up simple technique practices for short periods of time. In any case, controlled technical practice is a sensible way by which a games lesson can be brought to a close.

Continue for 5 minutes or a maximum of 10 minutes, if the practice goes well. The more skilful group should be subjected to challenge and competition in almost all practice activities.

Unit 2

Introductory Activity (5–10 minutes)

In 4's working across and outside the two square central channel. In fig. 109, B serves a ball on the bounce to A who volleys (hits the ball

Fig. 109

while it is in the air) to C. C controls and passes to D. D collects the ball and throws on the bounce to C so that C can return the sequence. As the players improve, the servers move around until the service is delivered from behind the volleyer.

Techniques to improve volleying:

Lean away from the ball when volleying it. The higher the ball the more you lean away to allow your kicking leg (and foot) to be raised higher. For a full overhead kick (volley), you fall backwards to enable your foot to be raised high enough to kick through the ball to keep the ball down. Concentrate your attention EXACTLY where you intend to strike the ball.

Kick by swinging your foot from your knee rather than from your hip.

Try to volley the ball so that the receiver does not have to move to control it.

Class Activity (15 minutes)

8 v 4, 7 v 5 or 6 v 6 practising Keep Ball. If this practice takes place in one half of a pitch, the use of space and therefore the use of longer kicks can be emphasized. Keep Ball played on one quarter of a pitch will demand:

1. tighter controlling skill.
2. greater skill in short, first time passing.

Match Practice or Game Form Activities (50 minutes)

12 v 12, 11 v 11 down to 9 v 9 on a full pitch.

Objectives:

1. to improve accuracy in passing and close control
2. to teach **penetration** as a principle of attack

The match times will be divided into four quarters or three thirds. Alternate periods, one and three or two and four, will be played under special conditions, the others will be played under normal ones. The following rules, any one of which can be applied, will help to emphasize the need for accuracy in passing:

1. All passes MUST be below knee height and MUST be to the feet of the target player—failure to comply with the conditions results in a free kick to the other team.

2. All passes MUST be delivered with the inside or the outside of the foot only.

3. Goals can be scored in the normal way AND by one team making ten consecutive passes without interruption.

The following rules will emphasize the need for close control:

1. A player may pass only AFTER he has touched the ball three times.

2. When not in possession of the ball a team must mark all opponents closely on a player to player basis.

The principle of penetration will be emphasized so that players understand the need to make forward passes when:

1. They can be delivered accurately.

2. The target player will have a reasonable chance to control the ball.

3. The target player will have supporting players near him when the pass arrives.

Technique Practice

In threes, 'one, two' passing—control with one foot and pass with the other. Build up as long an unbroken sequence as you can.

Unit 3

'B' GROUP

Introductory Activity

Here the class is divided into two ability groups. Group 'A' will be made up of the more skilful players.

On the coaching grid, in 4 squares, 4 v 2 practise Keep Ball. Score goals for the completion of set sequences of unbroken passes. e.g. 1 goal for 6 consecutive passes and so on.

Points to follow for Keep Ball game:

Select a target player.
Control the ball tightly.
Look away from your target player as if looking to pass to someone else.
Make the pass to your original target player.

Class Activity

Pressure practice—controlling techniques (fig. 110). In groups of 6, the servers take turns in throwing the ball to A who controls the ball and gives a return pass to the server. As the player in the centre becomes more skilful the servers, using a ball each, can serve the ball more quickly in succession. But never more than one ball at a time. The service must be controlled possibly even by the player under pressure.

Fig. 110

Game and Game Form Activity

6 v 6, Two Touch Football on a quarter pitch. Players must play the ball at least twice before passing.

Try to make opportunities for a wall pass or any return pass behind an opponent.

'A' GROUP

Introductory Activity

In 4 squares, 2 v 2 dribbling and shooting game (fig. 111). Attacking play takes place from each end alternately. Shoot when there is a clear line from your foot to the target (the goal).

Fig. 111

Class Activity

Defence v Attack. 6 defenders against 5 attackers in one half of the pitch. Attackers commence on the halfway line. The defending players are given specific opponents to mark or to shadow. The attackers change positions and try to lose their markers or their shadows.

Techniques for marking and shadowing.

When marking an opponent, a player must be between his opponent and the goal AND near enough to touch him. When shadowing an opponent a player must be between his opponent and his goal and far enough away to be able to see the opponent, the ball and be able to cover a nearby defender as well if necessary.

Game and Match Play

Objectives:
1. Delay in defence.
2. Intercepting and tackling.
   Try to 'guide' an opponent who has the ball away from goal. Try to force the opponent to move in the direction which you want him to take.
   When opponents have the ball take up positions so that when the ball is passed to a nearby opponent you can intercept it or make a tackle.

Unit 4

'B' GROUP

Introductory Activity and Class Activity

Divide the coaching grid into 2 pitches, each pitch is 40 yards (4 squares) × 30 yards (3 squares). The goals may be high jump stands or posts in bases 5 yards apart or mini goals. The group is divided into 4 teams, two teams to a pitch.

Game.
Team passing 6 v 6 using the following skills—volley kick, then control the ball in the air without using hands or arms and catch the ball. If a team fails to complete the sequence, possession of the ball

passes to the other side.

The team not in possession of the ball may intercept the ball or attempt to intercept the ball only AFTER the receiving player has made a controlling movement and is trying to catch the ball. Goals may be scored only by heading the ball or by volleying it.

Match Play

11 v 11 or 12 v 12—'All up all back'.

This match has one special rule in addition to the normal Laws of the Game. Before a team can score, all the team except the goal-keeper MUST be in their opponents' half of the pitch and before a team can play the ball forward out of its own defending half, all the team MUST be in that defending half.

Note the following points:

When in possession of the ball a team must take up positions where they can be seen by the player with the ball. When not in possession of the ball a team should be encouraged to mark opponents quickly and closely.

'A' GROUP

Introductory Activity

The whole class divides into pairs, one ball between two. Remaining inside the grid all the time, practise free dribbling to keep the ball. As one player loses the ball his opponent takes up the dribbling. After fixed, short periods of time ($\frac{1}{2}$ to 1 minute) stop the practice.

Which player has had possession of the ball most times?

Class Activity

Attack v Defence. The attackers start from the halfway line and the attacking team concentrates on taking up wide positions to have players as close to the touch lines as possible. If wing players move across the field, other players must take their places in these wide positions.

The defending team should be encouraged to watch for opponents taking up positions or moving behind defenders.

Game and Match Play

Objective:
1. Dispersal in attack
2. Attacking opponents with and without the ball
3. Marking and dodging

Whenever your team gains possession of the ball all players should spread themselves in all directions, over as much of the field as opponents will allow. You will find that it helps to take up a position on the far side of your nearest opponent, away from your team-mate who has the ball. This is known as the blind side. Your opponent will have difficulty watching you and the ball at the same time. Whenever you receive the ball try to attack the nearest opponent who is positioned between you and the opponent's goal. Run at him and past him. Similarly, if you do not have the ball and even if it is unlikely that you will receive it, be prepared to run past or behind nearby opponents. You will find that you can cause opponents to move in reaction to your movements. This is an important soccer skill. So is the skill of dodging a tight-marking opponent by changing the speed of your run, by stopping and starting, and not least by pretending to be doing one thing and doing something quite different!

Unit 5

'B' GROUP

Introductory Activity

Six players, in pairs, working in 4 squares on the grid. The goal is 8 yards wide. Play 2 v 2 football, 3 goals in. Whichever of the two playing teams scores 3 goals first, the losing team goes into goal and the two goalkeepers come out to continue 2 v 2 football.

Note the following points:

Any pass should result in a shot at goal (or the return pass should).
After giving a pass, move past one opponent (or both) to offer yourself for a return pass.

Class Activity

'Split' Football—the two teams are split into forwards and backs. Backs never move forward over the halfway line and forwards are never permitted to move back over the halfway line.

This game provides attack and defence practice.

Different combinations of backs and forwards will give opportunities for different forms of attack or defensive emphasis. e.g. 5 backs and 6 or 7 forwards. The backs, being outnumbered, have to defend together in all parts of their half. The forwards must try to exploit numerical advantage by switching the point of their attacking play. e.g. 6 backs v 5 forwards. In this situation the attackers must work hard to support each other in order to keep possession of the ball in order to make progress towards goal.

Game Form Activity.

12 v 12 or 11 v 11. A goal scored counts 3 points and any team which makes 10 uninterrupted passes scores 1 point.

This game emphasizes the importance of controlled possession of the ball.

'A' GROUP

Introductory Activity

In groups of 5 or 6, working in 6 squares on the coaching grid, 4 v 2 or 3 v 2, practise first time passing. What is the highest uninterrupted sequence of passes any group in possession can make?

Class Activity and Match Play

11 v 11 or 12 v 12. Emphasize the development of triangular play and triangle formations in defence and attack. The game will be stopped from time to time to emphasize the need for the triangle or show the benefits of the triangle.

Unit 6

Competition—Match Play

9 v 9 or 11 v 11 competitions. Match play with mixed and equally balanced teams.

A 4 team tournament will require 6 matches to be played and at 2 matches a week the tournament will take 3 weeks.

The Gold Star Super Skill tests can be used at any time to change the programme of activities. The scores recommended can be adjusted to test a player's skill at very high levels but the important thing to remember is that the tests and indeed the units of work recommended in this book are there to be used and adapted to suit the needs of young players who should not be used to meet the requirements of tests. This book has been written to help teachers who want to teach children; it so happens that soccer is the name of the game but children and their needs come first all the time.